Lose Your Belly Fat Cookbook

Lose Your BELLY FAT COOKBOOK

A Jump-Start Plan and 75 Delicious Recipes for Weight Loss

Alix Turoff, MS, RD, CDN, CPT

PHOTOGRAPHY BY OLIVIA BRENT

ROCKRIDGE PRESS

For general information on our other products and services or to obtain technical support, please contact our Customer Care Department within the U.S. at (866) 744-2665, or outside the U.S. at (510) 253-0500.

Rockridge Press publishes its books in a variety of electronic and print formats. Some content that appears in print may not be available in electronic books, and vice versa.

Interior and Cover Designer: Lisa Forde
Photo Art Director: Michael Hardgrove
Editor: John Makowski
Production Editor: Erum Khan
Photography © 2019 Olivia Brent.
Author photo courtesy of © NXM Photo.

Cover: Seared Sesame Ahi Tuna with Cabbage Slaw, pg. 105

ISBN: Print 978-1-64152-982-2 | eBook 978-1-64152-983-9

RO

This book is dedicated to my husband,
Sean, and to my mother, Victoria,
father, Reid, and sister, Tori.
And, of course, to my fur child, Oliver.

Contents

Introduction

If you're looking to jump-start your weight loss goals, targeting belly fat is a great place to start. When we think about belly fat, we often have aesthetic concerns in mind. But excess belly fat, specifically rooted, visceral fat, is also linked to a number of diseases, including type 2 diabetes, cardiovascular disease, and certain forms of cancer. Visceral fat is found inside the abdomen, and is stored around many organs, including the liver, pancreas, and intestines. It is typically controlled by diet and exercise. Although some body fat is necessary, visceral fat is a specific concern, and it's what we target when we talk about losing belly fat.

I became a registered dietitian because of my personal experience with weight loss. After years of losing and regaining weight through unhealthy and unsustainable methods, I enrolled in a clinical nutrition master's program at New York University and went on to become a registered dietitian. From there, I made it my life's goal to help people find a way to love and enjoy food for all the amazing things it provides, like community, joy, and comfort, without sacrificing their physical and mental health.

Over the years in private practice, I've helped countless clients lose weight and improve their health through diet and lifestyle changes. The true reward is when they call me to share their results from a most recent doctor's visit—not only have they lost weight but their lab results have also improved! My approach to nutrition is concerned with much more than just the number on a scale. My passion lies in helping clients regain their health so they can live long and happy lives . . . . Weight loss is just an added bonus.

When I work with clients, we begin to uncover unhealthy thinking patterns and behaviors that ultimately keep them trapped in the diet cycle. Through nutrition education and a little motivation, my clients repair their relationship with food so they can embrace a healthy lifestyle without self-sabotaging their efforts.

In this book, I provide a 14-day road map to improved health. The recipes you'll find in this book are not only delicious, but also designed and balanced in a strategic way to keep you full, provide sustained energy during your weight-loss journey, and offer variety to keep you motivated to stay the course.

Before you jump into the recipes, read the first two chapters where I explain the science and reasoning behind the jump-start plan. I'll also walk you through a few adjustments to your current lifestyle that you can make over the next two weeks.

This 14-day plan will serve as a great jump-start on your journey to better eating habits and a healthier lifestyle. Over the next 14 days, you'll reset your habits and likely lose a combination of both water and fat weight. More important, you'll feel great because you'll be eating nutrient-dense whole foods. This plan provides an appropriate balance of protein, fat, and carbohydrates to ensure you won't feel hungry, but you also won't experience the discomfort that results from overeating. The recipes in this book are easy to prepare, require minimal ingredients, and can be customized to suit your tastes.

Don't worry; your journey doesn't end after 14 days. With the resources in this book, you'll walk away feeling confident about your food choices and well equipped to make this a true lifestyle change—one that will help you slim down and regain your health.

I can't wait to give you the tools you need to transform your health and your relationship with food. Let's jump right in and start losing that belly!

PART 1

The Diet and Meal Plan

CHAPTER 1

The Diet

O ver the years, the word "diet" has developed a negative connotation, thanks in part to popular plans that eliminate entire food groups, utilize weeklong juice cleanses, and advise overly restrictive programs that expect followers to forgo their favorite foods in favor of bars and meal replacements. In reality, though, the word "diet" just describes a way of eating. It doesn't have to be punitive, rigorous, or miserable. In fact, once you understand the science behind weight loss, you'll be able to lose belly fat and decrease your risk for chronic disease—all while eating foods you love.

Why Is Belly Fat Such a Big Deal?

Waist circumference is one of the five risk factors for metabolic syndrome, which refers to a group of conditions including abdominal obesity, excess lipids in the blood, hypertension, and high blood sugar. When these occur together, they raise the risk of heart disease, stroke, and type 2 diabetes. Having excess belly fat, specifically visceral fat, has also been linked to chronic diseases, including some forms of cancer. Although we can't choose where we gain fat, we can control some lifestyle factors that may lead to a healthier fat distribution and a lower risk for chronic disease.

VISCERAL FAT VERSUS SUBCUTANEOUS FAT

Visceral fat is stored in the abdominal region and surrounds the liver, intestines, and pancreas. It's known as an "active" type of fat because of its ability to affect hormones. It's not visible, so it's possible, even at a healthy weight, that there is some hidden visceral fat in your abdomen.

Subcutaneous fat is the type of fat stored right below the skin. It's softer and more jiggly than visceral fat and is typically stored around the belly, thighs, and butt. It's more visible than visceral fat, but not nearly as dangerous.

How much belly fat do you really have?

The most accurate way to determine the amount of visceral fat is through a CT scan or MRI. These tests are extremely pricey and time-consuming, though, so your doctor is more likely to use waist circumference to get an idea of your overall visceral fat. A waist circumference equal to or greater than 40 inches in men and equal to or greater than 35 inches in women is considered abdominal obesity.

How Do I Get Rid of Belly Fat?

The program in this book is geared toward weight loss and emphasizes foods and behaviors that promote belly fat reduction. This diet is designed to help you lose weight while feeling full and satisfied. The suggested meals and snacks have a balance of protein, healthy fats, and complex carbohydrates. This plan will also increase your intake of dietary fiber, which is found in fruits, vegetables, legumes, nuts, seeds, and whole grains, and decrease your intake of added sugar, promoting the growth of healthy gut bacteria. This diet is not overly restrictive, as we know these types of diets don't last. Instead, you'll focus on eating a variety of healthy and delicious food in the right amounts.

The Macros

At the end of the day, weight loss comes down to "calories in" and "calories out," but that isn't to say the quality of your food doesn't matter. By following the strategic macronutrient breakdown in this book, we can ensure you feel full through the day, get an abundance of nutrients, and even have room for dessert.

HOW MANY CALORIES?

Our first step is to calculate your calorie needs for weight loss. This is a three-step process that you can do at home, but, if you have questions or concerns, your doctor or dietitian can guide you toward your specific needs.

Step 1: Calculate Your Basal Metabolic Rate (BMR)

Use the Mifflin-St. Jeor formula to calculate your BMR.

Men: $10 \times$ weight (kg) $+ 6.25 \times$ height (cm) $- 5 \times$ age (years) $+ 5$

Women: $10 \times$ weight (kg) $+ 6.25 \times$ height (cm) $- 5 \times$ age (years) $- 161$

Step 2: Calculate Your Total Daily Energy Expenditure (TDEE)

Take the number you got from Step 1 and multiply it by the appropriate activity factor.

Total Daily Energy Expenditure (TDEE) = BMR (from step 1) × Activity Factor

Activity Factors:

Sedentary (little or no exercise) = BMR × 1.15

Light activity (1 to 3 hours of exercise per week) = BMR × 1.2–1.35

Moderate activity (4 to 6 hours of exercise per week) = BMR × 1.4–1.55

Very active (7 to 9 hours of exercise per week) = MR × 1.6–1.75

Extra active (≥10 hours of exercise per week) = BMR × 1.8–1.95

Step 3: Calculate Your Daily Caloric Goal for Weight Loss

To lose weight, you need to be in a caloric deficit. For this program, we advise you start with a 20 percent deficit, which means you should eat about 80 percent of your TDEE to lose weight.

To figure this out, take your TDEE from Step 2 and multiply it by 80 percent.

For example, if your TDEE is 2,200 calories, your daily caloric goal would be 2,200 calories × 0.80, or about 1,760 calories per day.

Once you've calculated your daily caloric goal, you can then find your daily macronutrient recommendation. For your convenience, you can find your approximate macronutrient goals in the following table. Use the caloric goal that is closest to the number you calculated.

CALORIE GOAL	PROTEIN	FAT	CARBOHYDRATES
1,200 calories	90 g	40 g	120 g
1,500 calories	115 g	50 g	145 g
1,800 calories	135 g	60 g	180 g

NOTE: *Dietary fiber and sugar are both carbohydrates.*

Men should aim for 38 grams of fiber per day and less than 37.5 grams of added sugar.

Women should aim for 25 grams of fiber per day and less than 25 grams of added sugar.

PROTEIN

Protein is involved in many bodily functions including cellular maintenance and repair, blood clotting, and antibody production and it is a main component of many body tissues, including skin, hair, and muscles. Protein is digested more slowly than carbohydrates and, thus, helps you feel fuller longer. This diet encourages you to get 30 percent of your daily energy needs from protein.

Good sources of protein include:

- Chicken
- Cottage cheese
- Eggs
- Fish and shellfish
- Greek yogurt

- Lean beef
- Pork
- Tempeh
- Tofu
- Turkey

Protein reduces levels of the hunger hormone ghrelin, which stimulates appetite, so, by adding lean protein to your diet, you'll feel less hungry. Not only that, but protein has a higher thermic effect than fat or carbohydrates, meaning your body expends more energy digesting and metabolizing protein than it does fat or carbohydrates. Eating protein will not only help you feel fuller, because you won't feel your stomach growling, but it can actually help you burn *more* calories, too.

Speaking of protein . . .

When possible, choose a lean source of protein. According to the United States Department of Agriculture (USDA), a protein is considered lean if it has fewer than 10 grams of total fat, 4.5 grams or fewer of saturated fat, and fewer than 95 milligrams of cholesterol per 100-gram (3.5-ounce) portion. Fattier proteins should be limited, not only because of their excess calories, but also because a high percentage of saturated fat has been correlated to cardiovascular disease and other health issues.

Choose these protein sources that all contain about 25 to 35 calories per ounce most often.

Beef

- 96 percent lean ground beef
- Beef eye round roast
- Bottom round rump roast
- Eye round steak
- Filet mignon roast (beef loin roast)
- Flank steak
- Hanger steak
- Petite beef filet (beef shoulder steak)
- Top round London broil
- Top round steak
- Top sirloin

Fish and Seafood

- Black bass, Chilean sea bass, or striped bass
- Branzino
- Catfish
- Clams
- Cod
- Crab (crab legs, crabmeat, stone crab claws)
- Dorade
- Flounder
- Grouper
- Hake
- Halibut
- Lemon sole or Dover sole
- Lobster/lobster tails
- Mackerel
- Mahi-mahi
- Monkfish
- Mussels
- Octopus
- Oysters
- Perch
- Pollock
- Salmon (wild Alaskan sockeye, wild Coho)
- Salt cod

- Scallops

- Shrimp

- Snapper (wild)

- Tuna (wild yellowfin)

- Turbot

Pork

- 96 percent lean ground pork

- Boneless ham

- Canadian bacon

- Loin chops

- Pork loin roast

- Pork sirloin chops

- Pork tenderloin

Poultry (without skin)

- Chicken breast, leg, or thigh

- Ground chicken (more than 96 percent fat free)

- Ground turkey (more than 96 percent fat free)

- Quail breast

- Turkey bacon

- Turkey breast, leg, or thigh

Other red meat

- Bison rib eye steak

- Bison sirloin tip steak

- Bison steak tips

- Bison strip steak

- Leg of lamb cutlets

- Osso buco

- Veal leg cutlet

- Veal scaloppine

You don't need to eliminate red meat completely from your diet, as it contains an abundance of nutrients, but do limit the sources of red meat that are particularly high in saturated fat (such as short ribs, oxtail, rib eye, T-bone, porterhouse, strip steak, and skirt steak). Some studies have found a correlation between excess red meat consumption and type 2 diabetes and cardiovascular disease but, if you stick to leaner cuts, it can be enjoyed in moderation. If you eat red meat, choose an unprocessed source and limit your intake. I've included a few recipes using red meat for you to enjoy.

There are a number of sources of vegetarian protein that are either specialty products (specific brands of veggie burgers or meat substitutes) or are not pure protein (such as beans).

Tofu and tempeh are both vegetarian protein sources that can be counted as pure proteins—in other words, they are primarily protein and do not contain a significant amount of carbohydrates or fat. Tofu or tempeh can be substituted for a lean protein, if desired.

FATS

The idea that eating fat is off-limits is one whose time has passed. In fact, eating too little fat can impair hormone production and, ultimately, lead to binge eating. This diet encourages you to get 30 percent of your daily energy needs from fat to ensure you feel satisfied throughout the day. In general, focus on getting more of the "good" fats (the mono- and polyunsaturated fats, which include omega-3 fatty acids) and less of the "bad" fats (saturated and trans fats).

Good sources of fat include:

- Avocado
- Avocado oil
- Cheese
- Nuts and nut butter
- Oily fish (mackerel, salmon, sardines, trout)
- Olive oil
- Seeds (chia seeds, flaxseed, etc)
- Whole eggs

Omega-3 and omega-6 fatty acids are both essential, which means our bodies can't make them so we must get them from our diet. Flaxseed and flaxseed oil, chia seeds, walnuts and walnut oil, and fatty fish are all good sources of omega-3 fatty acids. Omega-6 fatty acids can be found in sunflower seeds and sunflower oil, pecans, Brazil nuts, and sesame oil. When looking at a food label, *avoid foods with high levels of saturated fat and avoid trans fats completely.* Be aware that some foods may contain small amounts of trans fats that are not listed on the label. To avoid taking in unwanted trans fats, avoid foods containing partially hydrogenated oils in the ingredient list.

CARBOHYDRATES

Losing weight doesn't have to mean cutting out carbohydrates. Instead of severely restricting carbohydrate intake, this diet emphasizes complex, high-fiber carbohydrates. When following this diet, you'll get about 40 percent of your daily caloric needs from carbohydrates. There are two main forms of carbohydrate: *complex* and *simple* carbohydrates.

Most of your daily carbohydrate intake should come from complex carbs. Good sources of complex carbs include:

- Fresh fruit
- Legumes
- Nonstarchy vegetables
- Oats
- Starchy vegetables (butternut squash, peas, sweet potatoes)
- Whole grains (barley, brown rice, quinoa)

Simple carbohydrates should be kept to a minimum and include foods such as:

- Baked goods
- Candy
- Dried fruit
- Fruit juice
- Potato chips
- Sugar, honey, agave nectar, and other added sweeteners
- White bread

When focusing on eliminating belly fat, choose carbohydrates high in dietary fiber and that have minimal added sugars.

FIBER

Fiber is the indigestible part of the carbohydrate. Humans lack the digestive enzymes needed to break it down, so it passes through the digestive tract unchanged. For this reason, fiber does not contribute calories to your diet. Fiber can also soak up water in the intestine, which slows the digestion of food and increases feelings of fullness, which can ultimately lead to a reduction in caloric intake. Fiber also plays an important role in regulating blood sugar. The more stable your blood sugar, the fewer cravings you'll have and the more satisfied you'll feel. Increasing your fiber intake can also improve digestion and regulate bowel movements, flushing out excess water and other unwanted digestive enzymes.

Fiber is found in plant-based foods including fruits, vegetables, legumes, and grains. Some types of fiber, known as prebiotic fibers, can also promote the growth of healthy gut bacteria. Prebiotic fibers provide the food the probiotic bacteria in the gut need to survive.

The two main types of fiber are *soluble* and *insoluble* fiber, and most plant foods have a combination. Adult men should aim to consume 38 grams and women 25 grams of total dietary fiber per day.

Soluble Fiber

Soluble fiber dissolves in water. It swells in your stomach and forms a gel, which can help you feel full by slowing digestion. It acts like a sponge, absorbing cholesterol and pulling it out of the body. It also plays a role in controlling blood sugar. Avocado, barley, carrots, legumes, oat bran, and sweet potatoes are all good sources of soluble fiber.

Insoluble Fiber

Insoluble fiber is sometimes referred to as "roughage" and does not dissolve in water. Insoluble fiber adds bulk to the stool, which can speed up the passage of food through the digestive tract. It aids in gastric motility (the muscle contractions that mash up your food into a liquid form), and may reduce the risk of colon cancer. Cauliflower, green beans, nuts, potatoes, and wheat bran are all good sources of insoluble fiber.

SUGAR

All sugar is not created equal. Added sugars do not occur naturally in foods and are *added* to foods during processing. Natural sugars are found in foods such as fruit, vegetables, and dairy products. Foods with added sugars are typically more processed, higher in overall calories, and lower in belly-filling fiber. Foods with natural sugars tend to have more fiber, vitamins, and minerals and are more likely to keep you full. The liver can convert added sugars into fat, ultimately increasing the amount of dangerous visceral fat. For this reason, added sugar should be limited to a daily intake of less than 37.5 grams for men and less than 25 grams for women.

Foods high in added sugars include:

- Baked goods (cakes, cookies, doughnuts)

- Candy

- Sugar-sweetened beverages (energy drinks, fruit juice, soft drinks)

The best way to avoid added sugar is to decrease your intake of processed and packaged foods.

It also helps to be a knowledgeable consumer. Food companies often use alternative names for sugar to confuse buyers.

Some of these alternative words for sugar are agave, cane juice and cane syrup, corn syrup, dextrose, fructose, honey, invert sugar, malt syrup, molasses, raw sugar, and maple syrup, to name a few.

Although many of these are okay in small amounts, pay attention to how many types of sugar and how much of each is in your food. Some companies will list multiple sugars in their ingredient lists (such as cane syrup, honey, and more) to avoid having to list sugar as the first ingredient.

When looking for added sugar, scan the ingredient list for anything ending in "-ose," such as dextrose or fructose. Another giveaway for added sugar is the word "syrup" or "juice." Always read your food labels!

Inflammation

Inflammation is the body's natural response to harm. When you get an infection or become injured, the body sends out chemicals that help ward off the infection and protect the injury. Although this type of inflammation is normal and natural, food can also cause inflammation in the body. Diets high in added sugar have been linked to higher levels of inflammation in the body. Not only can excess sugar trigger low-grade inflammation, it is also linked to elevated cholesterol, insulin resistance, and increased gut permeability, which can all trigger inflammation. When the gut is healthy, only certain things should pass through. When inflammation is present, the gut can become more permeable, allowing things to pass through that shouldn't. By reducing the amount of added sugar in your diet, you can avoid excess inflammation.

Whole Foods

The easiest way to practice and follow these guidelines is to eat whole, unprocessed foods. By doing this, you can easily avoid hidden sugars, extra calories, and ultra-processed ingredients. The goal of this program is to introduce you to an abundance of whole foods you will enjoy eating, which will make following this 14-day jump-start plan easy! You do not need to eat bland foods you dislike to lose weight. In fact, the key to long-term sustainable weight loss is finding foods you enjoy and look forward to eating every day.

Water, Caffeine, and Staying Hydrated

Water is involved in nearly every bodily process. Because we lose water daily through breathing, sweating, urinating, and bowel movements, constantly replenishing our water supply prevents dehydration. Not only will drinking enough water positively affect your energy levels, physical performance, and digestion, it can also aid in weight loss by increasing satiety and metabolic rate. Drinking water 30 minutes before meals can help you feel full and take in fewer calories.

The amount of water you need will depend on your body size, physical activity level, environment, and other factors. Ultimately, your body will do a good job of regulating your thirst by sending you signals to drink water when you need it. Some situations like exercise, breastfeeding, and heat call for increased water consumption. If you're sweating, it's a good sign you should drink more water to replace lost fluids.

A popular myth is that caffeinated beverages don't count toward your daily water intake but, in reality, caffeine may boost metabolism and improve brain function and mood. If you plan to consume caffeine, be mindful of what you add to it. For example, if you plan to enjoy coffee, be aware that adding sugar, cream, syrups, or milk can add a substantial number of calories. Choose lower-calorie mix-ins like almond milk to avoid consuming extra calories. If you plan to use a more caloric mix-in, such as heavy cream or half-and-half, keep portions small.

DRINKS TO AVOID

In general, avoid sugar-sweetened beverages like soda, fruit juice, sports drinks, and energy drinks. For weight loss, you should also be conscious of alcohol intake, but that doesn't mean you can't imbibe here and there. Opt for dry white or red wine over beer and choose spirits without sugary mixers. If you have a cocktail, trade the simple syrup and fruit juices for lemon, lime, or fresh muddled fruit. Or use club soda for a zero-calorie mixer.

There's really no nutritional definition of the word "superfood," though it's often used as a marketing term for foods rich in antioxidants, healthy fats, fiber, and other nutrients. Although the word itself might not mean much, there are certainly foods that provide significant amounts of nutrients, which may lead to improved health and weight loss. When choosing a snack, opt for one of these nutritionally dense foods in place of something with fewer nutrients and more calories. Although these foods are healthy, they do still contain calories, so be careful not to overdo them. Keep in mind that eating any of these foods won't magically erase something unhealthy you already ate; consider these new, nutrient-rich alternatives to your existing snacks.

Here are some "superfoods" to add to your diet:

Avocado: Avocado is a great source of monounsaturated fat, but it's also packed with fiber and potassium. Eating enough potassium may help maintain healthy blood pressure.

Berries: Berries are packed with antioxidants, which are associated with a reduced risk of cardiovascular disease, some cancers, and other inflammatory conditions. Blackberries and raspberries both pack 8 grams of fiber per 1-cup serving.

Dark leafy greens: Dark leafy greens are full of vitamins, minerals, and fiber. Just 1 cup of raw spinach provides 181 percent of your daily vitamin K needs and 56 percent of vitamin A.

Eggs: Eggs are considered one of the healthiest foods on the planet. Not only are they a great source of protein, but one egg yolk contains 113 mg of choline, an essential nutrient associated with heart and brain health and one that most adults do not get enough of.

Nuts and seeds: Nuts and seeds are a good source of plant-based protein and unsaturated fats. Just one Brazil nut provides more than a day's worth of selenium, which has antioxidant properties that can help protect the body from chronic disease.

Salmon: Salmon is not only a great source of protein, it's also one of the best sources of omega-3 fatty acids, which can reduce inflammation. Just one 3-ounce serving of salmon can provide all the omega-3 fatty acids you need for the day.

Gut Flora

There are trillions of microorganisms living in your gut. Although that might sound scary, more and more studies have solidified the link between the gut "microbiome" and overall health. The majority of bacteria live in the large intestine and a number of factors influence the types of bacteria found there. Genetics seem to influence the make-up of gut bacteria, which is unique to each person, but environmental and diet factors may also play a role. Recent studies have found that your gut bacteria may even influence your weight, affecting your appetite and the way your body breaks down food.

Foods thought to promote the growth of gut bacteria are generally low in calories and high in fiber, so they should be part of your diet already, but it doesn't hurt to make an effort to add these foods to your diet on a regular basis, especially because they're delicious!

FOODS THAT PROMOTE GUT BACTERIA

Consuming probiotic- and prebiotic-rich food is a great way to promote the growth of good bacteria. (Remember, *prebiotics provide the food for probiotics*.) Here are some food sources of each:

- Prebiotics: barley, garlic, Jerusalem artichokes, oats, onions, seaweed

- Probiotics: kefir, kimchi, miso, pickles, sauerkraut, tempeh, yogurt

SUPPLEMENTS

Although food is the preferred source of prebiotics and probiotics, they can also be taken as supplements. Consult your doctor before taking any supplement, as there are certain medical conditions for which they may not be warranted. Prebiotic and probiotic supplements can be found in most drugstores.

Calorie Deficit

As already stated, you must be in a calorie deficit to lose weight. Although the balance of macronutrients is important, ultimately, weight loss comes down to taking in fewer calories than you put out. This program is designed to help you stay in a calorie deficit without feeling hungry or restricted. The meals and recipes have a balance of macronutrients designed to keep you full, provide energy, and promote weight loss. If you are not losing weight, you may not be in a calorie deficit. Adjust your intake accordingly until you figure out the correct number of calories for your body and consult a doctor or RD if you're still having trouble.

PORTION SIZE

If you looked at a plate, would you feel comfortable identifying the portion of each food in front of you? If the answer is no, it might be time to purchase a food scale. Over time, you'll start to learn what a portion should look like and you won't need to rely on a food scale or measuring cups, but, in the beginning, these tools can be extremely helpful. Appropriate portion guidelines are given in the meal plan and recipes. Here are some helpful tips for estimating portion sizes:

Butter, condiments, and oil: 1 teaspoon = thumb tip

Cheese, nut butter, and salad dressing: 2 tablespoons = thumb

Dried fruit, nuts, and snacks: 1 ounce = handful

Fish, meat, poultry, and protein: 3 ounces = palm of your hand

Fruits, grains, pasta, and vegetables: 1 cup = closed fist

PLATE METHOD

A balanced plate should have a combination of protein, fat, and carbo-hydrates. When looking at your plate, aim to fill half with nonstarchy vegetables, one-quarter with lean protein, and one-quarter with a complex carbohydrate. Limit added fat to ½-tablespoon portion. Studies have found that by using smaller plates, you may consume less food without even realizing it. Your brain can take up to 20 minutes to recognize that you're full, so eating slowly can also help you decrease the amount of food you consume. You don't have to weigh and measure all your meals but doing so can help you to recognize what a proper serving size looks like.

Healthy, Sustainable Weight Loss

This diet is designed to promote healthy, safe, and sustainable weight loss, which means, on average, you can expect to lose 1 to 2 pounds per week, ultimately based on how much weight you have to lose. The more you have to lose, the faster your initial weight loss will be. By sticking with the caloric intake guidelines, you should avoid rapid weight loss, which is typically unsustainable and can even be unhealthy because of an insufficient number of calories and nutrients. When you lose weight too quickly, you risk damaging your metabolism, losing muscle mass, and getting into a cycle of binge eating. This program is meant to help you begin a new lifestyle and the recipes are designed to keep you full and satisfied while losing weight. When following this plan, you'll begin to form new healthy habits and behaviors, making this less of a "diet" in the traditional sense of the word and more of a long-term lifestyle.

WHAT TO EXPECT

After completing the 14-day plan, you can expect to have lost a combination of both water and fat. Not only will you be lighter, but you'll have more energy and improved digestion because you'll be eating the right amount of food for your body. This plan is meant to start you on a long-term journey to weight loss and optimal health.

SLIP-UPS

One important thing to remember as you embark on the next 14 days is that it's okay to slip up. Do your best to follow the plan but allow yourself flexibility. If you do go off course, acknowledge it and get right back on the plan.

Love Your Body

Although your body is likely to undergo changes during this process, it's important to able to love your body at all sizes. Weight loss may improve your physical health, but it won't necessarily make you happier. Enjoy and embrace this process and thank your body for all the amazing things it does for you every day.

Other Factors

Although food is one of the most important factors to control to lose belly fat, there are other factors that can help you achieve your goal.

SLEEP

Studies show that getting adequate sleep is strongly correlated with maintaining a healthy weight. Sleep deprivation can affect your hormones, which can lead you to eat more calories than your body needs. Not getting enough sleep can also negatively affect physical performance. Aim to get 7 to 9 hours of sleep per night.

Here are a few ways to ensure you get a restful night's sleep:

- Avoid caffeine after 12 p.m.

- Avoid using electronic devices, such as cell phones and laptops, in bed

- Create a bedtime schedule and stick to it, even on holidays and weekends

- Figure out what temperature is the most comfortable for you (70°F is good for most people)

STRESS

Stress is difficult to control and a certain amount of stress is normal. If you are particularly stressed, that can have a negative effect on your weight. Stress can increase cortisol levels in the body, which can interfere with weight loss when it's chronically elevated. Excess cortisol can lead to increased appetite and can signal the body to store fat. Some people respond to chronic stress with "stress eating" as a coping mechanism. This can lead to weight gain, which can increase stress further. If you find yourself stress eating, it's important to recognize this habit and replace it with a better coping mechanism, such as the ones that follow.

Managing your stress levels is crucial for living a healthy life. It's important to find ways to reduce stress in your life and you can do so without spending any money.

Here are a few free ways to de-stress:

- Aim to get 7 to 9 hours of sleep each night

- Exercise in moderate amounts

- Limit caffeine and alcohol intake

- Meditate

- Take a bath

But What About Exercise?

It's possible to lose weight without exercise, but regular physical activity is strongly correlated with chronic disease prevention. If you're not currently exercising, start with something small like taking a walk, doing a yoga video, or even signing up for a 5K race to get you motivated. Regular exercise, which maintains muscle mass, will help ensure your metabolism stays revved during the weight-loss process. Aerobic exercise, specifically, has been shown to reduce belly fat.

CHAPTER 2

The 14-Day Jump-Start Plan

The jump-start plan found in this book is a two-week program. It starts with a two-day smoothie cleanse, which is meant to reset the body and metabolism, and continues with 12 days of delicious food. You'll be eating up to six times a day, and each meal and snack is nutritionally balanced so you should never feel hungry.

The Two-Day Smoothie Cleanse

The first two days of your program involve a smoothie cleanse. This cleanse is meant to reset your body, mind, and metabolism and get you ready for the next 12 days. The smoothies are packed with protein, fiber, and healthy fats. You may feel hungry and notice you're craving sugar during the first two days. This is a normal part of adjusting to a new diet and your cravings should improve after the smoothie cleanse ends and subside by the end of Week 1. Drink plenty of water and avoid alcohol for the first two days.

Believe it or not, you can assemble your smoothies ahead of time. Gather all the ingredients you'll need, minus any liquid, and combine them in a freezer-safe glass jar (such as a mason jar). Store your prepped smoothies in the freezer and, when you're ready to make one, just add the contents of the jar and the liquid to a blender. Pour your smoothie right back in the same jar to take with you as you go about your day.

The Next 12 Days

After you follow the smoothie cleanse, you'll move on to the meal plan. The 12 days of the jump-start plan involve eating up to six times per day (three meals and three snacks).

- On the 1,200-calorie plan, you will eat 3 meals and 1 snack

- On the 1,500-calorie plan, you will eat 3 meals and 2 snacks

- On the 1,800-calorie plan, you will eat 3 meals and 3 snacks

Each day's menu is balanced in calories and macronutrients and is designed to model what a healthy eating day for weight loss looks like.

To succeed on this plan, follow the portions listed in the recipes. If a recipe says it serves four, you should split it into four portions and eat just one.

It will help to do some prep in advance. That might mean cooking eggs, cutting fruit, or marinating meat. Take time to read the recipes entirely so you are prepared.

If you plan to eat out or attend a social event over the 14-day jump-start, be mindful of your choices. Ideally, you'll limit alcohol over the next two weeks, but if you do plan to drink, try to limit yourself to one or two drinks per occasion, and eliminate one snack in exchange. If you're eating out, use the plate method described earlier (see page 22) to put together an appropriate meal. Aim to make half your plate vegetables, one-quarter lean protein, and one-quarter a high-fiber carbohydrate. You might not be able to control the types of food served at an event, but you can control your portions.

The Recipes

You will find 75 recipes in this book. All are easy to prepare with minimal ingredients that can be easily found at your local grocery store. These meals are designed to keep you full while you're in a calorie deficit.

Each recipe has the proper balance of calories and macronutrients. A small amount of minimal added sugar, like maple syrup or honey, is used in some recipes to enhance flavor. Eating well isn't about eating flavorless food! You can use small amounts of these ingredients to add flavor without overdoing it.

Not every recipe is used in the 14-day jump-start, so make sure to check them all out and try the rest on your own!

KEEP HEALTHY SNACKS NEARBY

On this plan, you will have up to three snacks per day, depending on your calorie goal.

- If you are following the 1,200-calorie plan, you will have 1 snack per day.

- If you are following the 1,500-calorie plan, you will have 2 snacks per day.

- If you are following the 1,800-calorie plan, you will have 3 snacks per day.

Your snacks should contain 150 to 200 calories with a nice balance of protein, fat, and carbohydrates. *Your snack should always be a combination of either carbohydrates and protein or carbohydrates and fat.* This will ensure that your snack keeps you full, satisfies your cravings, and regulates your blood sugar.

Here are some suggested snack pairings:

6 ounces 2% Greek yogurt + ¾ cup fresh berries

2 ounces turkey breast + 1 cup grapes

1 ounce nuts

1 ounce cheese + 2 pitted dates

½ ounce nuts + 1 banana

7 olives + 1 ounce cheese

2 hard-boiled eggs + ¼ avocado

1 apple + 1 tablespoon peanut butter

1 rice cake + 2 tablespoons hummus + 2 ounces turkey breast

1 whole-wheat pita + 2 tablespoons hummus

½ cucumber, sliced + 2 tablespoons soft goat cheese + 2 ounces smoked salmon

1 cup celery sticks + 2 tablespoons almond butter

1 cup raw vegetables + ¼ cup guacamole

½ cup 1% cottage cheese + 1 cup melon

⅓ cup part-skim ricotta + ½ cup fresh berries

FOODS YOU ENJOY

The key to long-term success in your healthy lifestyle is eating foods you enjoy. In any of the recipes, you can make equivalent substitutions according to your preferences. For example, if you see peanut butter in a smoothie, replace it with almond butter, if you prefer. If a recipe uses cauliflower but you like broccoli, replace that, too. Just be sure that the swaps are equivalent. If you want to replace a nonstarchy vegetable, such as mushrooms, swap in another nonstarchy veggie, not a starchy potato.

If you tend to get in a rut eating the same foods all the time, the next 14 days offer a chance to experiment with new flavors and combinations. Use the plan to try new things, introduce new recipes to your family, and have fun with new food choices.

Before you get started, record your weight and measurements. To track your progress, do this again after the 14-day plan and for 5 weeks thereafter. Please also note how you feel before and after following the plan.

	DAY 1	DAY 14	DAY 21	DAY 28	DAY 35	DAY 42	DAY 49
Weight							
Waist Circumference							
Upper Arm							
Chest							
Hips							
Upper Thigh							
Calves							
One a scale of 1 to 10, how good do you feel?							
On a scale of 1 to 10, how is your mood?							
On a scale of 1 to 10, how is your sleep?							

Before you get started, take some time to reflect on what you would like to get out of this experience. Do you want to feel better? Become more active? Increase your energy levels? Use the following prompts to gain clarity.

1. **What is currently holding you back from reaching your goals?**

   _____

   _____

   _____

2. **Where would you like to be six months from now regarding your health and fitness goals?**

   _____

   _____

   _____

3. **What are the things you tell yourself about why you can't achieve your goals?**

   _____

   _____

   _____

14-Day Jump-Start Plan

Note: This meal plan is designed to provide about 1,500 calories per day. If you are following the 1,200-calorie plan, **omit 1 snack** per day for a total of 3 meals and 1 snack.

If you are following the 1,800-calorie plan, **add 1 snack** per day for a total of 3 meals and 3 snacks.

You'll notice that the meal plan is designed with a lot of variety. That said, some people prefer to prep once and repeat meals, especially if they are following the plan by themselves. If you do this, be sure you're eating meals from the same category and adhering to proper portion guidelines. It can be helpful to store leftovers in individually portioned containers so you can quickly grab what you need without measuring.

For Day 1 and Day 2 of the smoothie cleanse, you can repeat the same smoothies both days. However, I've paired the smoothies such that your total macronutrients will be balanced for the day. If you want to have the same smoothies on Days 1 and 2, you can, but try to use one of the combinations mentioned.

If you prefer to choose your own meals, you can use these recipes interchangeably:

Breakfast
- Any recipe from the breakfast category
- Any recipe from the shakes and smoothies category

Lunch
- Strawberry and Watermelon Salad with Feta (page 85; add 4 ounces lean protein)
- White Bean Caprese Salad (page 81)
- Crunchy Cashew Thai Quinoa Salad (page 84)
- Cauliflower Rice Tabbouleh (page 83; add 4 ounces lean protein)
- BLT Chopped Salad (page 82)
- Any recipe from the Sandwiches and Wraps section (Greek Chicken Burgers [page 95] can be paired with Cauliflower Rice Tabbouleh [page 83], Black Bean and Corn Salad [page 80], or a 5-ounce potato)

Dinner
- Any recipe from the Mains section
- Any recipe from the Sandwiches or Wraps section plus 1 cup of a vegetable-based soup

MEAL PREP

Meal prep is an important skill, especially if you're adjusting to eating the majority of your meals at home. You can use the following template to figure out what to prep and when, based on the meals you choose and your weekly schedule. You might choose to prep full meals in advance, or save time by just getting your ingredients ready to go.

Here are some ideas to get you started:

- Cook your grains, such as quinoa or rice
- Make a big batch of a soup or stew ahead and freeze it in individual portions
- Trim and marinate your meat
- Use frozen meat options as long as they adhere to the lean protein guidelines
- Use frozen vegetables to save time and money
- Use rotisserie chicken without the skin where you can
- Wash and cut fruit and vegetables into the appropriate shapes

DAY	WHAT TO PREP
Sunday	
Monday	
Tuesday	
Wednesday	
Thursday	
Friday	
Saturday	

DAY #	BREAKFAST	SNACK	LUNCH	SNACK	DINNER
1 *Smoothie Cleanse*	1 Peanut Butter Banana Coffee Smoothie (page 66)	1 Tropical Anti-Bloat Smoothie (page 71)	1 Strawberry and Banana Smoothie (page 70)	1 Blueberry Cheesecake Smoothie (page 60)	1 Chocolate Almond Protein Smoothie (page 61)
2 *Smoothie Cleanse*	1 Chocolate Zucchini Smoothie (page 64)	1 Green Protein Smoothie (page 65)	1 Raspberry Yogurt Smoothie (page 69)	1 Vanilla Mango Smoothie (page 72)	1 Banana and Peanut Butter Tofu Smoothie (page 59)
3	1 Cinnamon Pear Cottage Cheese Bowls (page 53)	1 apple + 1 tablespoon peanut butter	1 Crunchy Cashew Thai Quinoa Salad (page 84)	1 cup raw vegetables + ¼ cup hummus	1 Sheet Pan Steak Fajitas (page 118)
4	1 Peanut Butter and Banana Sweet Potato Toast (page 54)	6 ounces 2% Greek yogurt + ¾ cup fresh berries	1 White Bean Caprese Salad (page 81)	1 ounce pistachios + 1 apple	1 Maple Dijon Sheet Pan Pork Chops (page 114)
5	1 Chocolate Avocado Smoothie (page 62)	1 cup raw vegetables + ¼ cup guacamole	1 Cauliflower Tofu Fried Rice (page 100)	1 ounce Swiss cheese + 2 pitted dates	1 Slow Cooker Lentil Chili (page 102)
6	1 Coconut Almond Hot Cereal (page 48)	1 ounce pistachios	1 Beef Barley Soup (page 115)	1 Grain-Free Chocolate Chunk Cookies (page 127)	1 Greek Spaghetti Squash with Shrimp (page 107)
7	1 Simple Shakshuka (page 55)	1 ounce mozzarella cheese + 2 pitted dates	1 White Chicken Chili (page 110)	1 Grilled Peaches with Ricotta and Honey (page 129)	1 Simple Shepherd's Pie (page 116)

DAY #	BREAKFAST	SNACK	LUNCH	SNACK	DINNER
8	1 Apple Cobbler Smoothie (page 58)	1 rice cake + 2 tablespoons hummus + 2 ounces turkey breast	1 Roast Beef Reuben Sandwich (page 97)	1 Peanut Butter Energy Balls (page 131)	1 Stuffed Peppers with Turkey and Brown Rice (page 113)
9	1 Apple Chia Overnight Oats (page 47)	⅓ cup part-skim ricotta + ½ cup fresh berries	1 Turkey Club Lettuce Wrap (page 96)	1 serving Savory Roasted Chickpeas (page 77)	1 Seared Sesame Ahi Tuna with Cabbage Slaw (page 105)
10	1 Peanut Butter and Oats Smoothie (page 68)	1 whole-wheat pita + 2 tablespoons hummus	1 Chicken Salad Cabbage Wraps (page 93)	1 ounce walnuts	1 Tuscan Pesto and White Bean Pasta (page 101)
11	1 High-Protein Avocado Toast (page 46)	1 ounce almonds + 1 banana	1 Tuna Salad Bell Pepper Sandwich (page 92)	1 Spicy Garlic Edamame (page 78)	1 Chicken Quinoa Enchilada Bake (page 111)
12	1 Chocolate Cauliflower Shake (page 63)	½ cucumber, sliced + 2 tablespoons soft goat cheese + 2 ounces smoked salmon	1 Chickpea Salad Pita Sandwich (page 89)	2 hard-boiled eggs + ¼ avocado	1 Salmon with Spinach and White Bean Orzo (page 103)
13	1 Cheesy Oats with Fried Eggs (page 49)	7 olives + 1 ounce cheese	1 Chicken Shawarma Bowl (page 112)	2 ounces turkey breast + 1 cup grapes	1 Greek Chicken Burgers (page 95) + 1 Cauliflower Rice Tabbouleh (page 83)
14	1 One-Pan Butternut Squash, Bacon, Eggs, and Brussels Sprouts (page 52)	1 cup celery sticks + 2 tablespoons almond butter	1 BLT Chopped Salad (page 82)	½ cup 1% cottage cheese + 1 cup chopped melon	1 Asian Chicken Lettuce Wraps (page 109)

CALORIE TRACKER

Use a calorie tracker to get an idea of how much you're eating.

Write down everything you eat for the day and note the calories and macronutrients for each food.

You can use the example on this page as a guide.

	QUANTITY/FOOD	CALORIES	FAT	CARBOHYDRATES	FIBER	PROTEIN
Breakfast	1 Slice Whole-Wheat Toast	90	1 g	18 g	2 g	4 g
	2 Eggs	150	10 g	0 g	0 g	12 g
	¼ Avocado	80	8 g	4 g	3 g	1 g
Snack						
Lunch						
Snack						
Dinner						
Snack						

When to Weigh Yourself

You should weigh yourself and take your measurements the morning of Day 1 and after Day 14. After the 14-day plan, I suggest weighing yourself daily to learn how your body weight fluctuates. Add your daily weights and average them to see your weekly weight loss.

Keep in mind that fluctuations on the scale are normal. There are a number of reasons the scale might be up, even when you're doing everything right. These are just a few reasons the scale might fluctuate:

You ate more sodium than usual.

You did strength training.

You drank less water than usual.

You're menstruating.

You ate your last meal later in the day than usual.

Regardless of what the scale says, keep going. If you stay consistent with diet and exercise, the results will come.

Non-Scale Victories

A non-scale gain, or victory, is the little "win" that comes along with eating well and living a healthy lifestyle. Sometimes the scale doesn't move, and during those times it's even more important to recognize these non-scale gains. Remember, eating well isn't only about weight loss; it's also about . . .

Being proud of yourself for following through on a commitment

Feeling good in your body

Fixing bad habits

Having more energy

Improving your emotional health and well-being (feeling less anxious, calmer, more confident)

The list goes on and on!

Remember to reflect regularly on your non-scale gains.

Beyond the Meal Plan

After the 14-day jump-start is over, you should remain on the diet going forward. Though this may sound daunting, there are many more delicious recipes in this book that will keep you on track and, as you get a better sense of macros and portions, you'll be able to seek out new favorites.

As you get used to eating this way, adjust the plan according to what's working for you. If you aren't losing weight, evaluate the number of calories you're consuming to get an idea of how much you're eating and whether you need to eat less. If you're losing more than 2 pounds per week, you may need to add a snack.

After Day 14, experiment with weighing yourself daily to learn how your body weight fluctuates. The scale might go up 3 pounds one day, which can be discouraging. If you weigh yourself daily, though, you'll see that same 3 pounds could be gone the next day. This is water weight and it's normal. You might find you don't lose weight every week, but you lose every other week. Once you start tracking your progress, you can identify trends.

Also experiment with different forms of exercise until you find something you like. Make it a point to move daily; even something as simple as going for a 10-minute walk can be effective.

Life will happen, but you can stay consistent. If you fall off track, just pick right back up with the next meal. The more you work on your diet, the easier it will become. Pretty soon, these healthy habits will be second nature!

PART II

The Recipes

CHAPTER 3

Breakfasts

High-Protein Avocado Toast

30 MINUTES, DAIRY-FREE, VEGAN

SERVES 4 / PREP TIME: 5 MINUTES

Avocado toast is like a blank canvas. You can top it with an egg, sprinkle it with feta cheese, or you can up the fiber and protein by adding beans, as in this recipe.

2 avocados, halved and pitted

1 cup canned chickpeas, drained and rinsed

1 tablespoon freshly squeezed lemon juice

½ teaspoon salt

4 slices whole-wheat bread, toasted

¼ cup hemp seeds

Red pepper flakes, for seasoning

Scoop the avocado flesh into a medium bowl. Add the chickpeas, lemon juice, and salt and mash together with a fork until well combined. It will be slightly lumpy. Divide the avocado-chickpea mixture among the toast slices. Sprinkle the toast with hemp seeds and red pepper flakes.

INGREDIENT TIP: Chickpeas are also known as garbanzo beans. If you don't have chickpeas, use white navy beans.

SUBSTITUTION TIP: If you are intolerant to gluten, you can use a gluten-free bread (check the label to ensure it was processed in a completely gluten-free facility). If you do not have a gluten intolerance, there's no reason to avoid gluten! Gluten-free products tend to have less fiber than traditional wheat products.

PER SERVING: Calories: 346; Total Fat: 20g; Protein: 12g; Carbohydrates: 33g; Sugars: 2g; Fiber: 11g; Sodium: 410mg

Apple Chia Overnight Oats

GLUTEN-FREE, ONE-POT, VEGETARIAN

SERVES 4 / PREP TIME: 5 MINUTES, PLUS 6 HOURS TO CHILL

This high-protein breakfast requires absolutely zero cooking time—perfect for meal prep! Any sweet apple, such as Fuji, Honeycrisp, Pink Lady, or Gala, will work.

2 cups plain nonfat Greek yogurt

1 cup unsweetened vanilla almond milk

1 teaspoon ground cinnamon

1 teaspoon vanilla extract

½ teaspoon salt

4 medium apples, cored and chopped

1 cup old-fashioned oats

¼ cup chia seeds

1. In a medium bowl or jar, combine the yogurt, almond milk, cinnamon, vanilla, and salt. Mix until smooth and well combined.

2. Stir in the apples, oats, and chia seeds. Cover the bowl and refrigerate for at least 6 hours (or overnight), until the oats are soft and have absorbed most of the liquid.

INGREDIENT TIP: If gluten sensitivity is a problem, always check the packaging to ensure ingredients were processed in a completely gluten-free facility.

PER SERVING: Calories: 338; Total Fat: 7g; Protein: 17g; Carbohydrates: 56g; Sugars: 28g; Fiber: 13g; Sodium: 376mg

Coconut Almond Hot Cereal

30 MINUTES, GLUTEN-FREE, ONE-POT, VEGETARIAN

SERVES 4 / PREP TIME: 5 MINUTES / COOK TIME: 5 MINUTES

Traditional oatmeal is fairly high in carbohydrates. By swapping out the oats for almond flour, you'll keep the carbohydrate content down while still enjoying a warm breakfast. This oatmeal alternative can be served hot or prepared in advance and enjoyed cold.

3 cups unsweetened vanilla almond milk

1 cup almond flour

½ cup unsweetened shredded coconut

¼ cup ground flaxseed

2 teaspoons ground cinnamon

1 tablespoon honey

1. In a medium saucepan over medium heat, combine the almond milk, almond flour, coconut, flaxseed, and cinnamon. Cook, for 3 to 5 minutes, whisking continuously until your desired thickness is reached.

2. Pour into four bowls and drizzle with honey to serve.

INGREDIENT TIP: If gluten sensitivity is a problem, always check the packaging to ensure ingredients were processed in a completely gluten-free facility.

STORAGE TIP: Refrigerate in an airtight container for up to 3 days.

PER SERVING: Calories: 273; Total Fat: 20g; Protein: 7g; Carbohydrates: 15g; Sugars: 6g; Fiber: 7g; Sodium: 148mg

Cheesy Oats with Fried Eggs

30 MINUTES, GLUTEN-FREE, VEGETARIAN

SERVES 4 / PREP TIME: 10 MINUTES / COOK TIME: 20 MINUTES

This recipe puts a savory spin on oatmeal, a traditionally sweet breakfast staple. By including spinach, cheese, and eggs, you add protein and fiber to help keep you full all morning.

Nonstick cooking spray

1 cup finely chopped yellow onion

4 garlic cloves, minced

Salt

Freshly ground black pepper

1⅓ cups old-fashioned rolled oats

4 cups water

2 cups cherry tomatoes, sliced

4 cups fresh baby spinach

4 large eggs

4 ounces reduced-fat Cheddar cheese, shredded

1. Place a small pot over medium-high heat and spray it with cooking spray. Add the onion and garlic and sauté for 2 to 3 minutes, or until the onion softens. Season with salt and pepper and stir to combine.

2. Stir in the oats. Add the water and reduce the heat to medium-low. Simmer the mixture for 10 to 12 minutes until the oats are tender, stirring occasionally to prevent them from burning.

3. While the oats cook, heat a medium skillet over medium heat and spray it with cooking spray. Add the tomatoes, cover the skillet, and cook for 5 minutes, shaking the pan occasionally to prevent the tomatoes from sticking.

4. When the tomatoes start to wrinkle, add the spinach. Cook, uncovered, for 2 to 3 minutes until the spinach wilts. Transfer the tomatoes and spinach to a plate and set aside.

5. Return the skillet to medium heat. Spray it again with cooking spray and fry the eggs to your liking.

6. Pour the oats into four bowls and top each with the tomato and spinach mixture and an egg. Evenly divide the Cheddar cheese among the bowls. Taste and season with salt and pepper, as needed.

INGREDIENT TIP: If gluten sensitivity is a problem, always check the packaging to ensure ingredients were processed in a completely gluten-free facility.

SUBSTITUTION TIP: You can substitute kale or Swiss chard for the spinach.

PER SERVING: Calories: 289; Total Fat: 13g; Protein: 20g; Carbohydrates: 27g; Sugars: 4g; Fiber: 5g; Sodium: 310mg

Mixed Berry Baked Oatmeal

GLUTEN-FREE, VEGETARIAN

SERVES 4 / PREP TIME: 5 MINUTES / COOK TIME: 30 MINUTES

Oatmeal starts many a day, but traditional oatmeal lacks the protein needed to keep you full. In this recipe, you'll use chia seeds, Greek yogurt, and egg whites to boost the protein. Make this baked oatmeal your own by swapping out the mixed berries for the fruit you prefer.

Nonstick cooking spray

2 cups old-fashioned rolled oats

¼ cup chia seeds

2 teaspoons ground cinnamon

1 teaspoon baking powder

¾ teaspoon salt

1 cup unsweetened vanilla almond milk

1 cup plain nonfat Greek yogurt

3 large egg whites

½ teaspoon vanilla extract

1½ cups mixed berries (raspberries and blueberries)

1. Preheat the oven to 350° F. Lightly coat an 8-by-8-inch baking dish with cooking spray.

2. In a large bowl, stir together the oats, chia seeds, cinnamon, baking powder, and salt.

3. Add the almond milk, yogurt, egg whites, and vanilla. Mix until combined.

4. Gently fold in the berries. Transfer the oat mixture to the prepared baking dish. Using a spatula, smooth the top.

5. Bake for 25 to 30 minutes, or until the top and edges are golden brown. Let cool before enjoying.

INGREDIENT TIP: If gluten sensitivity is a problem, always check the packaging to ensure ingredients were processed in a completely gluten-free facility.

SUBSTITUTION TIP: To make this egg free, use ⅓ cup unsweetened applesauce in place of the egg whites.

PER SERVING: Calories: 310; Total Fat: 8g; Protein: 18g; Carbohydrates: 44g; Sugars: 6g; Fiber: 13g; Sodium: 535mg

Avocado Egg Salad

30 MINUTES, GLUTEN-FREE, ONE-POT, VEGETARIAN

SERVES 3 / PREP TIME: 15 MINUTES

This is a great make-ahead recipe that can be eaten at breakfast or lunch. Serve it with high-fiber crackers for a filling and nutritious meal.

4 large hard-boiled eggs, peeled and chopped

1 avocado, peeled, pitted, and cut into ½-inch dice

2 tablespoons plain nonfat Greek yogurt

2 teaspoons white vinegar

1½ teaspoons finely chopped fresh chives

½ teaspoon salt

¼ teaspoon freshly ground black pepper

In a large bowl, combine the hard-boiled eggs, avocado, yogurt, vinegar, chives, salt, and pepper. Mix together and mash with a fork. Taste and season with more salt and pepper, as needed.

INGREDIENT TIP: If gluten sensitivity is a problem, always check the packaging to ensure ingredients were processed in a completely gluten-free facility.

PREPARATION TIP: Add some mustard to spice this up a bit, hummus for a little garlicky chickpea flavor, or hot sauce for some heat.

PER SERVING: Calories: 183; Total Fat: 15g; Protein: 9g; Carbohydrates: 6g; Sugars: 1g; Fiber: 4g; Sodium: 476mg

One-Pan Butternut Squash, Bacon, Eggs, and Brussels Sprouts

DAIRY-FREE, GLUTEN-FREE, ONE-POT

SERVES 4 / PREP TIME: 10 MINUTES / COOK TIME: 42 MINUTES

This sheet pan meal is packed with high-fiber vegetables and protein, and it makes a tasty and filling breakfast. With only one pan to clean, this recipe is a no-brainer.

Nonstick cooking spray

4 cups diced butternut squash

4 cups Brussels sprouts, trimmed and halved

1 tablespoon avocado oil

Salt

Freshly ground black pepper

4 turkey bacon slices, cut into 1-inch pieces

8 large eggs

1. Preheat the oven to 375° F. Spray a baking sheet with nonstick cooking spray.

2. On the prepared pan, combine the butternut squash, Brussels sprouts, and avocado oil. Season with salt and black pepper and toss to combine. Mix in the bacon.

3. Bake for 30 minutes.

4. Remove the pan from the oven and gently toss the vegetables, which should be fork-tender. Form 8 small "pockets" in the veggies with the back of a spoon and crack 1 egg into each pocket. Return the pan to the oven and bake for 10 to 12 minutes more until the whites are set.

5. Use a spatula to lift the eggs and veggie mixture from the pan and evenly divide among plates.

INGREDIENT TIP: If gluten sensitivity is a problem, always check the packaging to ensure ingredients were processed in a completely gluten-free facility.

SUBSTITUTION TIP: To make this dish vegetarian, omit the bacon and add ¾ cup canned beans.

PER SERVING: Calories: 279; Total Fat: 13g; Protein: 19g; Carbohydrates: 25g; Sugars: 6g; Fiber: 6g; Sodium: 371mg

Cinnamon Pear Cottage Cheese Bowls

30 MINUTES, GLUTEN-FREE, ONE-POT, VEGETARIAN

SERVES 4 / PREP TIME: 10 MINUTES

When you're sick of eggs but still want a protein-packed breakfast, cottage cheese comes to the rescue. This breakfast option is the perfect balance of savory and sweet.

3 cups 1% cottage cheese

4 pears, cored and sliced

¼ cup slivered almonds

1 tablespoon raw honey

½ teaspoon ground cinnamon

In a medium bowl, stir together the cottage cheese, pears, almonds, honey, and cinnamon until combined.

Divide among four bowls and serve.

INGREDIENT TIP: If gluten sensitivity is a problem, always check the packaging to ensure ingredients were processed in a completely gluten-free facility.

SUBSTITUTION TIP: Substitute Greek yogurt for the cottage cheese.

PER SERVING: Calories: 269; Total Fat: 5g; Protein: 23g; Carbohydrates: 36g; Sugars: 25g; Fiber: 6g; Sodium: 590mg

Peanut Butter and Banana Sweet Potato Toast

30 MINUTES, DAIRY-FREE, GLUTEN-FREE, ONE-POT, VEGAN

SERVES 4 / PREP TIME: 5 MINUTES / COOK TIME: 10 MINUTES

You may be thinking sweet potato and peanut butter sounds like a weird combination, but trust me, once you try it, you'll be hooked. If you prefer a savory breakfast, ditch the peanut butter and banana and go with avocado and tomato. And even better—the sweet potato IS the toast!

2 (5-ounce) medium sweet potatoes, ends trimmed, cut lengthwise into ¼-inch slices

½ cup peanut butter

2 bananas, sliced

Ground cinnamon, for garnish

1. Place the sweet potato slices into the toaster and toast for 2 to 3 cycles, until soft and starting to brown.

2. Place the toasted sweet potato slices on a plate and spread peanut butter on each. Top with sliced banana and sprinkle with cinnamon.

INGREDIENT TIP: If gluten sensitivity is a problem, always check the packaging to ensure ingredients were processed in a completely gluten-free facility.

PREPARATION TIP: If you do not have a toaster, set your oven to broil, place the sweet potatoes on a baking sheet, and broil for 4 to 6 minutes per side.

SUBSTITUTION TIP: Use almond butter or any seed butter in place of peanut butter.

PER SERVING: Calories: 302; Total Fat: 17g; Protein: 10g; Carbohydrates: 34g; Sugars: 13g; Fiber: 6g; Sodium: 187mg

Simple Shakshuka

30 MINUTES, DAIRY-FREE, GLUTEN-FREE, VEGETARIAN

SERVES 4 / PREP TIME: 5 MINUTES / COOK TIME: 25 MINUTES

Sometimes called "eggs in purgatory," shakshuka is a traditional dish popular in North Africa and throughout the Middle East. It's a delicious meal of baked eggs in a spicy tomato sauce. Some liken it to French ratatouille with an egg.

2 tablespoons olive oil

1 medium yellow onion, chopped

1 medium red bell pepper, chopped

2 garlic cloves, minced

1 teaspoon ground cumin

1 teaspoon smoked paprika

¼ teaspoon cayenne pepper

⅛ teaspoon salt

2 (14.5-ounce) cans low-sodium crushed tomatoes, with their juices

2 cups fresh basil, chopped

8 large eggs

1. In a large skillet over medium-high heat, heat the olive oil.

2. Add the onion and bell pepper and cook for about 2 minutes until soft.

3. Add the garlic, cumin, paprika, cayenne, and salt. Cook, stirring, for about 2 minutes until fragrant.

4. Lower the heat to medium and add the tomatoes and their juices.

5. Stir in the chopped basil. Simmer, uncovered, for 15 minutes, stirring occasionally.

6. Crack an egg into a small bowl. Using the back of a spoon, create a pocket in the tomato mixture large enough to fit the egg. Pour the egg into the pocket. Repeat with the remaining eggs. Cover the skillet and cook for 5 to 7 minutes until the eggs are set.

INGREDIENT TIP: If gluten sensitivity is a problem, always check the packaging to ensure ingredients were processed in a completely gluten-free facility.

PREPARATION TIP: The egg should be cooked similarly to a sunny-side up egg. Spice it up with hot sauce or harissa.

PER SERVING: Calories: 297; Total Fat: 16g; Protein: 17g; Carbohydrates: 23g; Sugars: 15g; Fiber: 8g; Sodium: 1,103mg

CHAPTER 4

Shakes and Smoothies

Apple Cobbler Smoothie

30 MINUTES, GLUTEN-FREE, ONE-POT, VEGETARIAN

SERVES 1 / PREP TIME: 5 MINUTES

Apple cobbler is not typically a breakfast food, but when you add cottage cheese for protein and oats for some healthy carbohydrates, you can get away with it. Any sweet apple, such as Fuji, Honeycrisp, Pink Lady, or Gala, will work. For more fiber, add ground flaxseed.

1 apple, peeled, cored, and chopped

¾ cup unsweetened vanilla almond milk

½ cup 1% cottage cheese

3 pitted dates

⅛ cup old-fashioned rolled oats

½ teaspoon ground cinnamon

In a high-speed blender, combine the apple, almond milk, cottage cheese, dates, oats, and cinnamon. Blend on high speed until smooth.

INGREDIENT TIP: If gluten sensitivity is a problem, always check the packaging to ensure ingredients were processed in a completely gluten-free facility.

STORAGE TIP: Refrigerate in a sealed mason jar for up to 24 hours. Shake well before drinking.

SUBSTITUTION TIP: To make this dairy free, use a dairy-free yogurt instead of the cottage cheese.

PER SERVING: Calories: 301; Total Fat: 4g; Protein: 17g; Carbohydrates: 53g; Sugars: 37g; Fiber: 5g; Sodium: 595mg

Banana and Peanut Butter Tofu Smoothie

30 MINUTES, DAIRY-FREE, GLUTEN-FREE, ONE-POT, VEGAN

SERVES 1 / PREP TIME: 5 MINUTES

Silken tofu is a soft, smooth form of tofu. It has a very mild taste, making it ideal for blending into sauces, dips, and smoothies. Unlike regular tofu, silken tofu is used to add creaminess to recipes. It's a great way to add some plant-based protein to your breakfast.

1 cup unsweetened vanilla almond milk

1 banana, frozen

4 ounces silken tofu

1 tablespoon peanut butter

1 tablespoon chia seeds

In a high-speed blender, combine the almond milk, banana, tofu, peanut butter, and chia seeds. Blend until smooth.

INGREDIENT TIP: If gluten sensitivity is a problem, always check the packaging to ensure ingredients were processed in a completely gluten-free facility.

SUBSTITUTION TIP: Use any nut or seed butter in place of the peanut butter.

PER SERVING: Calories: 378; Total Fat: 19g; Protein: 17g; Carbohydrates: 41g; Sugars: 18g; Fiber: 10g; Sodium: 298mg

Blueberry Cheesecake Smoothie

30 MINUTES, GLUTEN-FREE, ONE-POT, VEGETARIAN

SERVES 1 / PREP TIME: 5 MINUTES

Drinking this smoothie will make you feel like you're having dessert for breakfast. The only difference is you'll be getting tons of protein from the cottage cheese.

1 cup 1% cottage cheese

1 cup frozen blueberries

½ cup unsweetened vanilla almond milk

½ banana, frozen

¼ teaspoon ground cinnamon

In a high-speed blender, combine the cottage cheese, blueberries, almond milk, banana, and cinnamon. Blend until smooth.

INGREDIENT TIP: If gluten sensitivity is a problem, always check the packaging to ensure ingredients were processed in a completely gluten-free facility.

SUBSTITUTION TIP: Swap any type of berry for the blueberries.

PER SERVING: Calories: 320; Total Fat: 5g; Protein: 30g; Carbohydrates: 42g; Sugars: 28g; Fiber: 6g; Sodium: 600mg

Chocolate Almond Protein Smoothie

30 MINUTES, GLUTEN-FREE, ONE-POT, VEGETARIAN

SERVES 1 / PREP TIME: 5 MINUTES

Cacao nibs are small pieces of crushed cocoa beans. They're low in sugar, packed with vitamins, and add a nice crunch to your smoothie!

¾ cup plain nonfat Greek yogurt

½ cup unsweetened vanilla almond milk

1 banana, frozen

1 tablespoon almond butter

1½ teaspoons unsweetened cocoa powder

2 teaspoons cacao nibs

1. In a high-speed blender, combine the yogurt, almond milk, banana, almond butter, and cocoa powder. Blend until smooth.

2. Pour into a glass and top with the cacao nibs.

INGREDIENT TIP: If gluten sensitivity is a problem, always check the packaging to ensure ingredients were processed in a completely gluten-free facility.

SUBSTITUTION TIP: Use any nut or seed butter you prefer.

PER SERVING: Calories: 362; Total Fat: 13g; Protein: 26g; Carbohydrates: 44g; Sugars: 23g; Fiber: 9g; Sodium: 155mg

Chocolate Avocado Smoothie

30 MINUTES, GLUTEN-FREE, ONE-POT

SERVES 1 / PREP TIME: 5 MINUTES

Putting avocado in a smoothie may sound unusual, but it adds a ton of creaminess and texture. Paired with nut butter, this smoothie will keep you full and satisfied for hours.

1 cup unsweetened vanilla almond milk

1 serving chocolate protein powder

1 cup fresh baby spinach

¼ avocado, peeled

1 tablespoon almond butter

In a high-speed blender, combine the almond milk, protein powder, spinach, avocado, and almond butter. Blend until smooth.

INGREDIENT TIPS: When choosing a protein powder, look for one with less than 140 calories per serving and about 20 grams of protein. If you can, opt for a whey protein isolate. If you follow a vegan or dairy-free diet, opt for a plant-based protein powder.

If gluten sensitivity is a problem, always check the packaging to ensure ingredients were processed in a completely gluten-free facility.

SUBSTITUTION TIP: Use any nut or seed butter you prefer.

PER SERVING: Calories: 327; Total Fat: 20g; Protein: 26g; Carbohydrates: 14g; Sugars: 4g; Fiber: 7g; Sodium: 398mg

Chocolate Cauliflower Shake

30 MINUTES, GLUTEN-FREE, ONE-POT

SERVES 1 / PREP TIME: 5 MINUTES

Adding frozen cauliflower to your shake makes it extra creamy and you won't even taste it. It's the perfect way to sneak some veggies into your (or your kid's!) breakfast.

1 cup unsweetened vanilla almond milk

1 cup frozen cauliflower florets

1 serving chocolate protein powder

½ banana, frozen

1½ tablespoons cocoa powder

1 tablespoon almond butter

In a high-speed blender, combine the almond milk, cauliflower, protein powder, banana, cocoa powder, and almond butter. Blend until smooth.

INGREDIENT TIPS: If you follow a vegan or dairy-free diet, opt for a plant-based protein powder.

If gluten sensitivity is a problem, always check the packaging to ensure ingredients were processed in a completely gluten-free facility.

VARIATION TIP: Make it mocha by replacing half the almond milk with chilled coffee.

PER SERVING: Calories: 401; Total Fat: 20g; Protein: 33g; Carbohydrates: 43g; Sugars: 13g; Fiber: 16g; Sodium: 372mg

Chocolate Zucchini Smoothie

30 MINUTES, GLUTEN-FREE, ONE-POT

SERVES 1 / PREP TIME: 10 MINUTES

If you've never had zucchini in a smoothie, be prepared for a surprise. This veggie makes your smoothie extra creamy without sacrificing the chocolate flavor.

1 cup unsweetened vanilla almond milk

½ medium zucchini, chopped and frozen

½ banana, frozen

½ serving chocolate protein powder

1 tablespoon almond butter

1 tablespoon cocoa powder

2 teaspoons cacao nibs

1. In a high-speed blender, combine the almond milk, zucchini, banana, protein powder, almond butter, and cocoa powder. Blend until smooth.

2. Pour into a glass and top with the cacao nibs.

INGREDIENT TIPS: If you follow a vegan or dairy-free diet, opt for a plant-based protein powder.

If gluten sensitivity is a problem, always check the packaging to ensure ingredients were processed in a completely gluten-free facility.

SUBSTITUTION TIP: Use any nut or seed butter you prefer.

PER SERVING: Calories: 344; Total Fat: 19g; Protein: 21g; Carbohydrates: 38g; Sugars: 12g; Fiber: 14g; Sodium: 271mg

Green Protein Smoothie

30 MINUTES, GLUTEN-FREE, ONE-POT

SERVES 1 / PREP TIME: 5 MINUTES

This smoothie might look green, but you'd never know it by the way it tastes! It's sweet, creamy, and packed with protein and vitamins.

½ cup unsweetened vanilla almond milk

½ cup vanilla nonfat Greek yogurt

½ serving vanilla protein powder

1½ cups fresh baby spinach

½ cup frozen pineapple chunks

½ cup frozen raspberries

½ green apple, peeled, cored, and chopped

In a high-speed blender, combine the almond milk, yogurt, protein powder, spinach, pineapple, raspberries, and apple. Blend until smooth.

INGREDIENT TIP: If gluten sensitivity is a problem, always check the packaging to ensure ingredients were processed in a completely gluten-free facility.

SUBSTITUTION TIP: To make this smoothie vegan, omit the Greek yogurt and use one full serving of plant-based protein powder.

PER SERVING: Calories: 398; Total Fat: 2g; Protein: 24g; Carbohydrates: 77g; Sugars: 62g; Fiber: 11g; Sodium: 211mg

Peanut Butter Banana Coffee Smoothie

30 MINUTES, DAIRY-FREE, GLUTEN-FREE, ONE-POT, VEGAN

SERVES 1 / PREP TIME: 10 MINUTES

With this smoothie, you get your caffeine boost and breakfast all in one glass. Talk about efficient!

1 banana, frozen

½ cup coffee, chilled

½ cup unsweetened vanilla almond milk

¼ cup old-fashioned rolled oats

1 tablespoon peanut butter

In a high-speed blender, combine the banana, coffee, almond milk, oats, and peanut butter. Blend until smooth.

INGREDIENT TIP: If gluten sensitivity is a problem, always check the packaging to ensure ingredients were processed in a completely gluten-free facility.

SUBSTITUTION TIP: Use any nut or seed butter you prefer.

PER SERVING: Calories: 294; Total Fat: 11g; Protein: 8g; Carbohydrates: 45g; Sugars: 17g; Fiber: 7g; Sodium: 166mg

Peanut Butter and Jelly Protein Shake

30 MINUTES, GLUTEN-FREE, ONE-POT, VEGETARIAN

SERVES 1 / PREP TIME: 5 MINUTES

This shake is a high-protein twist on a childhood classic—the only thing missing is the bread.

¾ cup plain nonfat Greek yogurt

½ cup unsweetened vanilla almond milk

½ cup frozen raspberries

½ cup frozen strawberries

1 tablespoon peanut butter

In a high-speed blender, combine the yogurt, almond milk, raspberries, strawberries, and peanut butter. Blend until smooth.

INGREDIENT TIP: If gluten sensitivity is a problem, always check the packaging to ensure ingredients were processed in a completely gluten-free facility.

SUBSTITUTION TIP: Use any nut or seed butter you prefer.

PER SERVING: Calories: 271; Total Fat: 10g; Protein: 24g; Carbohydrates: 26g; Sugars: 17g; Fiber: 7g; Sodium: 227mg

Peanut Butter and Oats Smoothie

30 MINUTES, DAIRY-FREE, GLUTEN-FREE, ONE-POT, VEGAN

SERVES 1 / PREP TIME: 5 MINUTES

Don't have time to sit down to a bowl of oatmeal? Take this nutrition-packed smoothie with you on the go!

½ cup unsweetened vanilla almond milk

½ banana, frozen

¼ cup old-fashioned rolled oats

2 tablespoons peanut butter

1 tablespoon ground flaxseed

In a high-speed blender, combine the almond milk, banana, oats, peanut butter, and flaxseed. Blend until smooth.

INGREDIENT TIP: If gluten sensitivity is a problem, always check the packaging to ensure ingredients were processed in a completely gluten-free facility.

SUBSTITUTION TIP: Use any nut or seed butter you prefer.

PER SERVING: Calories: 373; Total Fat: 21g; Protein: 13g; Carbohydrates: 36g; Sugars: 11g; Fiber: 8g; Sodium: 241mg

Raspberry Yogurt Smoothie

30 MINUTES, GLUTEN-FREE, ONE-POT, VEGETARIAN

SERVES 1 / PREP TIME: 5 MINUTES

Per serving, raspberries (and blackberries) have more fiber than any other fruit (8 grams in 1 cup!). When you pair them with chia seeds and flaxseed, you can get nearly half your daily fiber in one smoothie.

1 cup unsweetened vanilla almond milk

1 cup frozen raspberries

½ cup plain nonfat Greek yogurt

½ banana, frozen

1 tablespoon ground flaxseed

1 tablespoon chia seeds

In a high-speed blender, combine the almond milk, raspberries, yogurt, banana, flaxseed, and chia seeds. Blend until smooth.

INGREDIENT TIP: If gluten sensitivity is a problem, always check the packaging to ensure ingredients were processed in a completely gluten-free facility.

SUBSTITUTION TIP: Blackberries also pack a ton of fiber per serving. You can swap them for raspberries or mix the two together. If you don't like banana, use ½ cup frozen mango or pineapple instead.

PER SERVING: Calories: 329; Total Fat: 11g; Protein: 19g; Carbohydrates: 43g; Sugars: 19g; Fiber: 17g; Sodium: 228mg

Strawberry and Banana Smoothie

30 MINUTES, GLUTEN-FREE, ONE-POT

SERVES 1 / PREP TIME: 5 MINUTES

This five-ingredient smoothie is not only delicious, but also packed with protein. You can buy frozen strawberries or make your own! If you have any fresh strawberries that are about to go bad, chop off the leaves and stems, and freeze the berries in a sealable plastic bag for future use.

1 cup unsweetened vanilla almond milk

¾ cup frozen strawberries

1 serving vanilla protein powder

½ banana, frozen

1 tablespoon chia seeds

In a high-speed blender, combine the almond milk, strawberries, protein powder, banana, and chia seeds. Blend until smooth.

INGREDIENT TIPS: If you follow a vegan or dairy-free diet, opt for a plant-based protein powder.

If gluten sensitivity is a problem, always check the packaging to ensure ingredients were processed in a completely gluten-free facility.

STORAGE TIP: Refrigerate in a sealed mason jar for up to 48 hours. Shake well before drinking.

PER SERVING: Calories: 306; Total Fat: 8g; Protein: 27g; Carbohydrates: 35g; Sugars: 18g; Fiber: 9g; Sodium: 243mg

Tropical Anti-Bloat Smoothie

30 MINUTES, DAIRY-FREE, GLUTEN-FREE, ONE-POT, VEGAN

SERVES 1 / PREP TIME: 5 MINUTES

Rough weekend? Start your Monday with this smoothie! Pineapple contains an enzyme called bromelain, which can aid in protein digestion and reduce bloating and swelling.

½ cup unsweetened vanilla almond milk

½ cup frozen mango chunks

½ cup frozen pineapple chunks

½ cup fresh baby spinach

½ cucumber, chopped

¼ cup fresh mint leaves

1 tablespoon chia seeds

In a high-speed blender, combine the almond milk, mango, pineapple, spinach, cucumber, mint, and chia seeds. Blend until smooth.

INGREDIENT TIP: If gluten sensitivity is a problem, always check the packaging to ensure ingredients were processed in a completely gluten-free facility.

NUTRITION TIP: For more protein, add hemp seeds or a scoop of vanilla protein powder.

SUBSTITUTION TIP: Use frozen papaya in place of the mango or pineapple.

PER SERVING: Calories: 215; Total Fat: 7g; Protein: 6g; Carbohydrates: 38g; Sugars: 23g; Fiber: 11g; Sodium: 116mg

Vanilla Mango Smoothie

30 MINUTES, GLUTEN-FREE, ONE-POT, VEGETARIAN

SERVES 1 / PREP TIME: 5 MINUTES

One cup of mango provides almost 70 percent of your daily vitamin C needs. Fresh mango can be tricky to cut, but using frozen mango makes it easy to enjoy this antioxidant-rich fruit.

1 cup vanilla nonfat Greek yogurt

½ cup unsweetened vanilla almond milk

1 cup frozen mango chunks

1 tablespoon chia seeds

In a high-speed blender, combine the yogurt, almond milk, mango, and chia seeds. Blend until smooth.

INGREDIENT TIP: If gluten sensitivity is a problem, always check the packaging to ensure ingredients were processed in a completely gluten-free facility.

SUBSTITUTION TIP: Try frozen papaya or pineapple instead of the mango for a different tropical taste.

PER SERVING: Calories: 368; Total Fat: 7g; Protein: 23g; Carbohydrates: 60g; Sugars: 50g; Fiber: 8g; Sodium: 199mg

Snacks and Salads

High-Protein Deviled Eggs

30 MINUTES, GLUTEN-FREE, ONE-POT, PESCATARIAN

SERVES 4 / PREP TIME: 20 MINUTES

Traditional deviled eggs are very high in fat because of all that mayo. This version is still creamy, thanks to the unsaturated fats in the avocado, but is also high in filling protein and lower in fat. Plus, avocados are a healthy fat that should be part of your regular diet.

---

1 avocado, halved and pitted

2 (6-ounce) cans solid white albacore tuna in water, drained and rinsed

¼ cup plain nonfat Greek yogurt

4 scallions, green and white parts, chopped

Salt

Freshly ground black pepper

6 large hard-boiled eggs, halved lengthwise, yolks removed and saved for another use

1 teaspoon paprika

6 mini cucumbers, sliced, for serving

1. Scoop the avocado flesh into a medium bowl. Add the tuna, yogurt, and scallions and season with salt and pepper. Mix and mash well with a fork. Spoon the tuna mixture into the egg white halves.

2. Sprinkle with paprika and serve with cucumber slices on the side.

INGREDIENT TIPS: Sprinkle the leftover egg yolks on salads or mix them with some Greek yogurt, a dash of mustard, salt, and pepper for a quick egg salad that will keep in the refrigerator for up to 5 days.

If gluten sensitivity is a problem, always check the packaging to ensure ingredients were processed in a completely gluten-free facility.

SUBSTITUTION TIP: For a vegetarian version, replace the tuna with ⅓ cup white beans or chickpeas, mashed.

PER SERVING: Calories: 236; Total Fat: 8g; Protein: 31g; Carbohydrates: 12g; Sugars: 4g; Fiber: 4g; Sodium: 390mg

Savory Roasted Chickpeas

30 MINUTES, DAIRY-FREE, GLUTEN-FREE, VEGAN

SERVES 4 / PREP TIME: 5 MINUTES / COOK TIME: 25 MINUTES

Roasted chickpeas are a great way to satisfy a craving for something salty and crunchy. You can use any seasoning you'd like to suit your tastes. To make them extra crispy, dry the chickpeas completely before seasoning them.

1 (15-ounce) can chickpeas, drained and rinsed

1 tablespoon olive oil

½ teaspoon paprika

½ teaspoon ground cumin

½ teaspoon salt

¼ teaspoon freshly ground black pepper

¼ teaspoon garlic powder

¼ teaspoon onion powder

1. Preheat the oven to 400° F. Line a baking sheet with parchment paper.

2. Spread the chickpeas on paper towel and pat them dry. Transfer the chickpeas to a large bowl and add the olive oil, paprika, cumin, salt, pepper, garlic powder, and onion powder. Mix to combine, making sure the chickpeas are evenly coated. Spread the chickpeas in a single layer on the prepared baking sheet.

3. Bake for 20 to 25 minutes, tossing halfway through the baking time, until crispy.

INGREDIENT TIP: If gluten sensitivity is a problem, always check the packaging to ensure ingredients were processed in a completely gluten-free facility.

STORAGE TIP: Refrigerate the chickpeas in an airtight container for up to 5 days. If they become less crunchy over time, bake them in a 400° F oven for a few minutes before eating.

PER SERVING: Calories: 134; Total Fat: 5g; Protein: 6g; Carbohydrates: 18g; Sugars: 3g; Fiber: 5g; Sodium: 296mg

Spicy Garlic Edamame

30 MINUTES, DAIRY-FREE, ONE-POT, VEGAN

SERVES 4 / PREP TIME: 5 MINUTES / COOK TIME: 10 MINUTES

Edamame, or immature green soybeans, are popular in Asian cuisine. They are high in both fiber and protein and make a great snack or side dish. You can find edamame in the frozen section of the grocery store.

½ teaspoon sesame oil

4 garlic cloves, minced

1 tablespoon chile paste

1 tablespoon low-sodium soy sauce

2 cups frozen edamame, in pods

1 tablespoon sesame seeds, for garnish

1. Bring a large pot of salted water to boil over high heat.

2. In a small skillet over medium-low heat, heat the sesame oil. Add the garlic and sauté for 3 minutes until the garlic begins to brown. Remove the skillet from the heat and let cool.

3. Stir the chile paste and soy sauce into the garlic. Set aside.

4. Add the edamame to the boiling water and cook for 6 minutes. Drain well and pat dry. Add the warm edamame to the garlic chili sauce and toss to coat.

5. Garnish with sesame seeds and serve.

SUBSTITUTION TIP: To make this recipe gluten free, use tamari or coconut aminos in place of the soy sauce.

PER SERVING: Calories: 97; Total Fat: 5g; Protein: 6g; Carbohydrates: 8g; Sugars: 2g; Fiber: 2g; Sodium: 201mg

Spinach Yogurt Dip with Caramelized Onions

30 MINUTES, GLUTEN-FREE, VEGETARIAN

SERVES 4 / PREP TIME: 5 MINUTES / COOK TIME: 15 MINUTES

Spinach yogurt dip, or *borani esfenaj* in Farsi, is a traditional Persian appetizer. It's typically served with a Persian flatbread called *barbari,* but it's delicious with naan, pita chips, or crudités as well.

1½ teaspoons olive oil

1 large sweet onion, sliced

4 cups fresh baby spinach

1 garlic clove, minced

1 cup plain nonfat Greek yogurt

Salt

Freshly ground black pepper

¼ cup walnuts, chopped

1. In a large skillet over medium heat, heat the olive oil.

2. Add the onion and cook for 5 to 7 minutes until it begins to caramelize. Add the spinach and turn the heat to low. Cook for 2 to 3 minutes until the spinach wilts. Stir in the garlic and cook for 2 minutes more. Transfer the spinach to a large bowl to cool.

3. Once the spinach mixture is cooled, add the yogurt. Stir to mix. Taste and season with salt and pepper, as needed.

4. Sprinkle with chopped walnuts and serve.

INGREDIENT TIPS: Frozen spinach will work in this recipe. However, if you use frozen spinach, squeeze it well to get rid of any excess water.

If gluten sensitivity is a problem, always check the packaging to ensure ingredients were processed in a completely gluten-free facility.

PREPARATION TIP: This dip tastes even better when it's made 1 to 2 days in advance. Complete steps 1 through 3, then refrigerate the dip in a sealed container. Before serving, stir well and sprinkle with chopped walnuts.

PER SERVING: Calories: 144; Total Fat: 10g; Protein: 5g; Carbohydrates: 9g; Sugars: 6g; Fiber: 2g; Sodium: 102mg

Black Bean and Corn Salad

30 MINUTES, DAIRY-FREE, GLUTEN-FREE, VEGAN

SERVES 4 / PREP TIME: 10 MINUTES

This salad is full of different flavors and textures. It can be served as a side dish or used as a topping for fish, chicken, or steak. It even makes a great dip!

FOR THE DRESSING

2 teaspoons olive oil

2 tablespoons freshly squeezed lime juice

2 teaspoons agave nectar

¾ teaspoon chili powder

¾ teaspoon ground cumin

Salt

Freshly ground black pepper

FOR THE SALAD

1½ cups canned black beans, drained and rinsed

1 mango, diced

1 avocado, peeled, pitted, and cubed

1 red bell pepper, diced

1 cup corn kernels

1 jalapeño pepper, diced

½ cup chopped fresh cilantro

¼ cup diced red onion

TO MAKE THE DRESSING

In a small bowl, whisk together the olive oil, lime juice, agave, chili powder, and cumin. Taste and season with salt and pepper. Whisk again. Set aside.

TO MAKE THE SALAD

1. In a large bowl, combine the black beans, mango, avocado, red bell pepper, corn, jalapeño, cilantro, and red onion.

2. Pour the dressing over the bean mixture and gently toss to coat. Serve chilled or at room temperature.

INGREDIENT TIPS: Any kind of corn will work in this recipe: canned, frozen (thawed), or fresh, cut from the cob.

If gluten sensitivity is a problem, always check the packaging to ensure ingredients were processed in a completely gluten-free facility.

STORAGE TIP: This salad tastes even better when it's made a day in advance. It will keep refrigerated, in an airtight container, for up to 5 days.

PER SERVING: Calories: 295; Total Fat: 10g; Protein: 9g; Carbohydrates: 47g; Sugars: 19g; Fiber: 12g; Sodium: 57mg

White Bean Caprese Salad

30 MINUTES, GLUTEN-FREE, ONE-POT, VEGETARIAN

SERVES 4 / PREP TIME: 15 MINUTES

This salad is the perfect recipe for Meatless Monday. The beans and mozzarella cheese provide protein—and you don't even need to turn on the stove.

4 cups canned cannellini beans or chickpeas, drained and rinsed

2 cups cherry tomatoes, diced

4 ounces fresh mozzarella cheese, cubed

½ teaspoon minced garlic

1 cup fresh basil, chopped

Salt

Freshly ground black pepper

1 tablespoon olive oil

¼ cup balsamic vinegar

In a large bowl, combine the beans, tomatoes, mozzarella, garlic, and basil. Season with salt and pepper and mix well to combine. Drizzle the salad with olive oil and vinegar. Gently toss. Serve cold.

INGREDIENT TIP: If gluten sensitivity is a problem, always check the packaging to ensure ingredients were processed in a completely gluten-free facility.

STORAGE TIP: If you want to make this salad in advance, mix all the ingredients except the olive oil and vinegar. Refrigerate the bean mixture it an airtight container and drizzle with oil and vinegar when you're ready to serve.

PER SERVING: Calories: 361; Total Fat: 11g; Protein: 23g; Carbohydrates: 45g; Sugars: 3g; Fiber: 14g; Sodium: 225mg

BLT Chopped Salad

30 MINUTES, GLUTEN-FREE, ONE-POT

SERVES 4/ PREP TIME: 10 MINUTES

This recipe turns a classic sandwich, the BLT, into a salad. Adding corn, avocado, feta, and savory Green Goddess Dressing will keep you full for hours—you won't even notice there's no bread.

8 cups chopped butter lettuce

2 cups quartered cherry tomatoes

8 turkey bacon slices,
cooked and crumbled

1 cup corn kernels

1 avocado, peeled, pitted, and cubed

1 cup crumbled feta cheese

½ cup Green Goddess Dressing (page 135)

In a large bowl, combine the lettuce, tomatoes, bacon, corn, avocado, and feta cheese. Mix well. Add the dressing and toss to coat.

INGREDIENT TIPS: Any kind of corn will work in this recipe: canned, frozen (thawed), or fresh, cut from the cob.

If gluten sensitivity is a problem, always check the packaging to ensure ingredients were processed in a completely gluten-free facility.

SERVING TIP: Top with Savory Roasted Chickpeas (page 77) for a nice crunch!

PER SERVING: Calories: 327; Total Fat: 22g; Protein: 16g; Carbohydrates: 21g; Sugars: 6g; Fiber: 7g; Sodium: 750mg

Cauliflower Rice Tabbouleh

30 MINUTES, DAIRY-FREE, GLUTEN-FREE, ONE-POT, VEGAN

SERVES 4 / PREP TIME: 15 MINUTES

This recipe puts a low-carbohydrate spin on tabbouleh, which is traditionally made with bulgur wheat.

4 cups riced cauliflower

3 cups fresh parsley, finely chopped

1 cup fresh mint leaves, finely chopped

2 tomatoes, diced

1 cucumber, diced

½ cup minced scallion, green and white parts

Juice of 1 lemon

2 tablespoons olive oil

2 tablespoons red wine vinegar

Salt

Freshly ground black pepper

In a large bowl, combine the cauliflower, parsley, mint, tomatoes, cucumber, and scallion. Gently stir to combine. Add the lemon juice, olive oil, and vinegar and toss until well combined. Taste and season with salt and pepper, as needed.

INGREDIENT TIPS: You can buy cauliflower already in rice form (fresh or frozen), or you can make your own. Cut one cauliflower head into florets, add them to a food processor or blender, and pulse until you achieve a rice-like texture.

If gluten sensitivity is a problem, always check the packaging to ensure ingredients were processed in a completely gluten-free facility.

PER SERVING: Calories: 143; Total Fat: 8g; Protein: 6g; Carbohydrates: 18g; Sugars: 6g; Fiber: 7g; Sodium: 108mg

Crunchy Cashew Thai Quinoa Salad

30 MINUTES, DAIRY-FREE, VEGAN

SERVES 4 / PREP TIME: 20 MINUTES

Not only is this salad beautiful, it's also delicious. You can add shrimp, chicken, or tofu for an even more filling meal.

FOR THE DRESSING

¼ cup smooth peanut butter

3 tablespoons low-sodium soy sauce

2 teaspoons grated peeled fresh ginger

1 tablespoon agave nectar

1 tablespoon rice wine vinegar

1 teaspoon sesame oil

2 tablespoons water (optional)

FOR THE SALAD

1 cup cooked quinoa

2 cups shredded purple cabbage

1 red bell pepper, diced

¼ cup diced red onion

1 cup shredded carrots

½ cup chopped fresh cilantro

½ cup cashew halves

6 scallions, green and white parts, chopped

1 lime, cut into wedges

TO MAKE THE DRESSING

In a medium microwave-safe bowl, heat the peanut butter in the microwave for 20 seconds. Remove from the microwave and stir in the soy sauce, ginger, agave, vinegar, and oil, stirring until the mixture is smooth. If you like a thinner dressing, stir in the water, 1 teaspoon at a time, until you reach your desired consistency.

TO MAKE THE SALAD

1. In a large bowl, combine the quinoa, cabbage, pepper, onion, carrots, and cilantro. Mix to combine. Add the dressing and toss to coat.

2. Garnish with cashews and scallions and serve with lime wedges for squeezing. Serve chilled or at room temperature.

STORAGE TIP: If you do not plan to serve this right away, do not dress the salad until 1 to 2 hours before you are ready to serve. Both the dressing and the salad can be kept in the refrigerator for up to 5 days. If needed, reheat the dressing in a microwave-safe bowl to thin it.

SUBSTITUTION TIP: To make this gluten free, substitute tamari for the soy sauce.

PER SERVING: Calories: 349; Total Fat: 19g; Protein: 12g; Carbohydrates: 38g; Sugars: 11g; Fiber: 6g; Sodium: 488mg

Strawberry and Watermelon Salad with Feta

30 MINUTES, GLUTEN-FREE, VEGETARIAN

SERVES 4 / PREP TIME: 15 MINUTES

This is the perfect salad to serve at any summer party. It's light, refreshing, and holds up well in the heat. The sweet flavors of the strawberry and watermelon contrast perfectly with the savory feta and salty pistachios.

FOR THE DRESSING

1 tablespoon honey

Juice of 1 lemon

¼ cup balsamic vinegar

1 tablespoon olive oil

⅛ teaspoon salt

⅛ teaspoon freshly ground black pepper

FOR THE SALAD

2 cups fresh strawberries, hulled and sliced

2 cups cubed seedless watermelon

1 cucumber, diced

½ cup chopped fresh mint leaves

½ cup crumbled feta cheese

¼ cup shelled pistachios, chopped

TO MAKE THE DRESSING

In a small mason jar, combine the honey, lemon juice, vinegar, olive oil, salt, and pepper. Cover the jar and shake to combine. Set aside.

TO MAKE THE SALAD

In a large bowl, combine the strawberries, watermelon, cucumber, mint, feta, and pistachios. Add the dressing and gently stir to combine. Serve cold.

INGREDIENT TIP: If gluten sensitivity is a problem, always check the packaging to ensure ingredients were processed in a completely gluten-free facility.

PREPARATION TIP: Add black olives and/or thinly sliced red onion for a flavor boost.

PER SERVING: Calories: 175; Total Fat: 9g; Protein: 5g; Carbohydrates: 21g; Sugars: 15g; Fiber: 3g; Sodium: 279mg

CHAPTER 6

Sandwiches and Wraps

Cheesy Black Bean Quesadilla

30 MINUTES, ONE-POT, VEGETARIAN

SERVES 4 / PREP TIME: 10 MINUTES / COOK TIME: 5 MINUTES

These cheesy black bean quesadillas come together in 15 minutes and make the perfect weeknight dinner. Serve them with a side salad for a full meal.

---

2 cups canned black beans, drained and rinsed

1 cup corn kernels

½ cup chopped red onion

4 ounces reduced-fat Cheddar cheese, shredded

¼ teaspoon garlic powder

¼ teaspoon cayenne pepper

¼ teaspoon ground cumin

2 teaspoons freshly squeezed lime juice

Salt

Freshly ground black pepper

4 small whole-wheat tortillas

Nonstick cooking spray

½ cup fresh cilantro, for garnish (optional)

1. In a large bowl, combine the beans, corn, onion, and Cheddar cheese. Gently stir to mix.

2. Add the garlic powder, cayenne, cumin, and lime juice and season with salt and pepper. Stir until well mixed.

3. Place the tortillas on a work surface.

4. Evenly divide the bean mixture among the tortillas, placing the filling on one side of each tortilla. Fold the other side of the tortilla over the filling.

5. Coat a large skillet with cooking spray and place it over medium-low heat. Add the quesadillas and cook for 1 to 2 minutes per side until they begin to brown and the cheese melts.

6. Garnish with cilantro (if using).

INGREDIENT TIP: Any kind of corn will work in this recipe: canned, frozen, or fresh, cut from the cob.

SERVING TIP: Serve with fresh salsa, guacamole, or your desired toppings.

STORAGE TIP: To freeze the quesadillas, prepare as directed, then place them on a baking sheet lined with parchment paper. Place the baking sheet in the freezer for 1 hour until the quesadillas freeze, then transfer them to a freezer bag. To reheat the quesadillas, microwave them or cook in a skillet over low heat, until warm. They will keep in the freezer for up to 2 months.

PER SERVING: Calories: 372; Total Fat: 12g; Protein: 20g; Carbohydrates: 50g; Sugars: 3g; Fiber: 12g; Sodium: 367mg

Chickpea Salad Pita Sandwich

30 MINUTES, DAIRY-FREE, VEGAN

SERVES 4 / PREP TIME: 10 MINUTES

If you're looking for a plant-based alternative to chicken salad, you've come to the right place! This chickpea salad is packed with protein and fiber and makes a great weekday lunch.

1 (15-ounce) can chickpeas, drained and rinsed

2 celery stalks, diced

⅓ cup chopped red bell pepper

2 scallions, green and white parts, chopped

½ cup grapes, sliced

3 tablespoons hummus

1 tablespoon Dijon mustard

1 teaspoon freshly squeezed lemon juice

Salt

Freshly ground black pepper

4 whole-wheat pitas

1. Place the chickpeas in a large bowl and mash them with a fork.

2. Add the celery, bell pepper, scallions, and grapes and stir to combine.

3. In a small bowl, stir together the hummus, mustard, and lemon juice and season with salt and pepper. Pour the hummus mixture over the chickpea salad and gently toss to coat.

4. Lightly toast the pitas and fill each with chickpea salad.

PREPARATION TIP: You can mash the chickpeas or leave them whole. I prefer them mashed but still slightly lumpy for a nice texture.

STORAGE TIP: Refrigerate the chickpea salad in an airtight container for 3 to 4 days.

PER SERVING: Calories: 326; Total Fat: 5g; Protein: 13g; Carbohydrates: 59g; Sugars: 10g; Fiber: 11g; Sodium: 416mg

Make-Ahead Spinach Goat Cheese Wraps

30 MINUTES, VEGETARIAN

SERVES 4 / PREP TIME: 10 MINUTES / COOK TIME: 20 MINUTES

Store-bought frozen foods are convenient, but they don't always have the healthiest (or tastiest) ingredients. Make these wraps ahead of time and stash them in the freezer for a healthy, grab-and-go lunch for busy weekdays.

4 large eggs

6 large egg whites

Nonstick cooking spray

Salt

Freshly ground black pepper

1 teaspoon olive oil

4 cups fresh baby spinach

1 cup cherry tomatoes, halved

4 large tortillas

4 ounces crumbled goat cheese

1. In a large bowl, whisk the eggs and egg whites until well combined.

2. Place a large skillet over medium heat and coat it with cooking spray.

3. Pour the eggs into the skillet. Cook for 3 to 5 minutes, stirring occasionally, or until the eggs are cooked to your desired doneness. Season with salt and pepper and transfer to a plate to cool.

4. Return the skillet to medium heat and heat the olive oil. Add the spinach and tomatoes and cook for 2 to 3 minutes until the spinach wilts. Remove the spinach and tomatoes from the skillet and set aside to cool.

5. Place the tortillas on a work surface. Evenly distribute the eggs, spinach, tomatoes, and goat cheese down the middle of each tortilla. Tightly wrap them like a burrito. Serve immediately, or place the wraps in a large freezer-safe storage bag and freeze until ready to eat.

6. To reheat, microwave on high power for 2 minutes.

INGREDIENT TIP: Using liquid egg whites in this recipe makes for easier cleanup and no waste.

PER SERVING: Calories: 369; Total Fat: 16g; Protein: 22g; Carbohydrates: 31g; Sugars: 3g; Fiber: 5g; Sodium: 538mg

Smoked Salmon Nori Roll-Ups

30 MINUTES, GLUTEN-FREE, PESCATARIAN

SERVES 4 / PREP TIME: 10 MINUTES

You can buy nori in the international aisle of your grocery store. If you have any left after you make these roll-ups, nori makes a great crunchy snack!

4 large nori sheets, cut down the middle

2 avocados, pitted, peeled, and sliced

1 cucumber, thinly sliced

1 red bell pepper, thinly sliced

12 ounces smoked salmon

¼ cup cream cheese, at room temperature

1. Place the nori sheets on a work surface.

2. Evenly divide the avocado, cucumber, bell pepper, salmon, and cream cheese among the sheets. Wrap and enjoy.

INGREDIENT TIP: If gluten sensitivity is a problem, always check the packaging to ensure ingredients were processed in a completely gluten-free facility.

PREPARATION TIP: Add wasabi or ginger for an extra blast of flavor.

PER SERVING: Calories: 325; Total Fat: 22g; Protein: 20g; Carbohydrates: 13g; Sugars: 3g; Fiber: 8g; Sodium: 1,758mg

Tuna Salad Bell Pepper Sandwich

30 MINUTES, GLUTEN-FREE, PESCATARIAN

SERVES 4 / PREP TIME: 10 MINUTES

If you've ever made a tuna salad sandwich, you know that the bread can become soggy. Skip the soggy bread and the extra carbs by making a bell pepper sandwich instead. The pepper adds a nice crunchy bite.

4 (6-ounce) cans solid white albacore tuna in water, drained and rinsed

4 celery stalks, diced

⅔ cup diced red onion

⅔ cup shredded carrots

½ cup plain nonfat Greek yogurt

¼ cup hummus

2 tablespoons white vinegar

Salt

Freshly ground black pepper

2 bell peppers, any color, halved, seeded, and ribs removed

1. Place the tuna in a large bowl. Add the celery, onion, carrots, yogurt, hummus, and vinegar. Using a fork, mix until well combined then season with salt and pepper.

2. Evenly distribute the tuna salad among each bell pepper half and serve.

INGREDIENT TIP: If gluten sensitivity is a problem, always check the packaging to ensure ingredients were processed in a completely gluten-free facility.

PREPARATION TIP: This is a great opportunity to try a salad chopper or a mezzaluna in a wooden bowl.

SUBSTITUTION TIP: Use mustard or avocado in place of the yogurt or hummus for an extra burst of flavor.

PER SERVING: Calories: 228; Total Fat: 7g; Protein: 30g; Carbohydrates: 12g; Sugars: 6g; Fiber: 3g; Sodium: 636mg

Chicken Salad Cabbage Wraps

30 MINUTES, GLUTEN-FREE

SERVES 4 / PREP TIME: 10 MINUTES / COOK TIME: 10 MINUTES

Traditional chicken salad can be highly caloric, due in part to the copious amounts of mayonnaise and, in some versions, dried fruit. This lightened-up version uses Greek yogurt to maintain a creamy texture without the extra unhealthy fat.

1 teaspoon avocado oil

1 pound boneless, skinless chicken breast, cubed

½ teaspoon dried thyme

2 celery stalks, chopped

½ apple, diced

½ cup plain nonfat Greek yogurt

1 tablespoon red wine vinegar

1 teaspoon freshly squeezed lemon juice

Salt

Freshly ground black pepper

1 head purple cabbage, cored, leaves separated

1. In a large skillet over medium heat, heat the avocado oil. Add the chicken and thyme. Cook for 6 to 8 minutes, stirring occasionally, until the chicken is cooked through. Transfer to a large bowl.

2. Add the celery and apple to the bowl and toss to combine.

3. In a small bowl, stir together the yogurt, vinegar, and lemon juice. Add the dressing to the chicken mixture and mix well to coat. Season with salt and pepper.

4. Wrap the chicken mixture in cabbage leaves to serve.

INGREDIENT TIPS: If you prefer, serve this chicken salad romaine or butter lettuce leaves.

If gluten sensitivity is a problem, always check the packaging to ensure ingredients were processed in a completely gluten-free facility.

SERVING TIP: Enjoy the remaining ½ apple as a snack paired with 1 Peanut Butter Energy Ball (page 131).

STORAGE TIP: Refrigerate in an airtight container for up to 4 days.

SUBSTITUTION TIP: To make this dairy free, substitute hummus or avocado for the yogurt.

PER SERVING: Calories: 207; Total Fat: 3g; Protein: 32g; Carbohydrates: 14g; Sugars: 9g; Fiber: 5g; Sodium: 185mg

Grilled Chicken Caesar Wrap

30 MINUTES

SERVES 4 / PREP TIME: 15 MINUTES

Caesar salad is delicious, but traditional Caesar dressing has loads of calories per serving. By making your own dressing, you can enjoy all the flavor of a Caesar salad without taking in excess fat. Make this lunch even easier by using a pre-cooked rotisserie chicken from the grocery store!

4 sandwich-size whole-wheat wraps

½ cup Light Caesar Dressing (page 136)

1 pound grilled chicken breasts, diced

2 cups shredded romaine lettuce

¼ cup grated Parmesan cheese

1. Place the wraps on a work surface. Spread 2 tablespoons of the dressing in an even layer over each wrap.

2. Top with the chicken, lettuce, and Parmesan cheese. Roll up the wraps tightly and serve.

STORAGE TIP: If you're not serving these right away, keep the dressing on the side and wrap the sandwich in foil. Refrigerate until you're ready to eat, and serve with the dressing as a dipping sauce.

PER SERVING: Calories: 405; Total Fat: 16g; Protein: 39g; Carbohydrates: 31g; Sugars: 3g; Fiber: 4g; Sodium: 1,417mg

Greek Chicken Burgers

30 MINUTES

SERVES 4 / PREP TIME: 10 MINUTES / COOK TIME: 20 MINUTES

You can prep these burgers in advance so that when you come home after a busy day all you have to do is throw them on the grill. When choosing ground chicken, look for at least 96 percent lean.

1 pound extra-lean ground chicken breast

2 cups fresh baby spinach, finely chopped

½ cup chopped red onion

½ cup crumbled feta cheese

1 teaspoon dried oregano

½ teaspoon salt

4 whole-wheat buns, toasted

1. Preheat the grill to medium heat.

2. In a medium bowl, stir together the chicken, spinach, onion, feta, oregano, and salt until well combined. Form the mixture into 4 patties.

3. Place the patties on the grill and cook for 8 to 10 minutes per side, or until cooked through and no longer pink.

4. Serve the burgers on toasted buns with your favorite toppings.

PREPARATION TIP: If you don't have a grill, use a large nonstick skillet to cook the burgers.

SERVING TIP: Serve with tomato and/or cucumber slices and Green Goddess Dressing (page 135).

STORAGE TIP: If you plan to freeze these for more than 1 week, wrap them individually in plastic wrap and aluminum foil to prevent freezer burn.

PER SERVING: Calories: 310; Total Fat: 7g; Protein: 33g; Carbohydrates: 28g; Sugars: 5g; Fiber: 5g; Sodium: 732mg

Turkey Club Lettuce Wrap

30 MINUTES, GLUTEN-FREE

SERVES 4 / PREP TIME: 10 MINUTES

A diner favorite with a twist! The crispy romaine lettuce adds the perfect crunch to this quick lunch.

1 head romaine lettuce, leaves separated

1 avocado, peeled, pitted, and sliced

1 pound cooked turkey breast, sliced

8 turkey bacon slices, cooked

4 (1-ounce) slices Swiss cheese

8 slices tomato

1. Place 4 (14-by-14-inch) pieces of parchment paper on a work surface.

2. Layer one-quarter of the large lettuce leaves in the middle of each piece of parchment to create a base.

3. Place one-quarter of the avocado in the center of the lettuce, then layer each with equal amounts of the turkey, bacon, Swiss cheese, and tomato.

4. Starting with the end closest to you, roll each lettuce wrap as tightly as possible, using the parchment paper to help, tucking the ends of the wrap toward the middle halfway through. Tightly roll the rest of the parchment tightly around the lettuce wrap.

5. Use a serrated knife to cut the lettuce wrap across the middle, but do not cut all the way through; leave a small piece of parchment intact to hold the wrap together. Repeat with the remaining wraps.

INGREDIENT TIPS: Use butter lettuce or kale in place of the romaine lettuce.

If gluten sensitivity is a problem, always check the packaging to ensure ingredients were processed in a completely gluten-free facility.

SUBSTITUTION TIP: To make this dairy free, omit the cheese and add more avocado.

PER SERVING: Calories: 385; Total Fat: 23g; Protein: 35g; Carbohydrates: 13g; Sugars: 4g; Fiber: 2g; Sodium: 726mg

Roast Beef Reuben Sandwich

30 MINUTES, ONE-POT

SERVES 4 / PREP TIME: 5 MINUTES / COOK TIME: 5 MINUTES

A traditional Reuben sandwich is made with corned beef and Russian dressing. Corned beef is cured with salt, so substituting roast beef helps reduce the sodium content without sacrificing flavor.

8 slices rye bread

¼ cup yellow mustard, divided

4 (1-ounce) slices Swiss cheese

1 cup sauerkraut, drained

1 pound roast beef, sliced

Nonstick cooking spray

1. Place 4 slices of bread on a work surface. Spread each slice with 1 tablespoon of mustard.

2. Top with the Swiss cheese, sauerkraut, roast beef, and the remaining 4 slices of bread.

3. Heat a large skillet over medium heat and coat it with cooking spray.

4. Place the sandwiches in the skillet and cook both sides until golden brown and the cheese begins to melt. Serve hot.

PREPARATION TIP: If you have a sandwich press, preheat it and cook the sandwiches in the press for 3 to 5 minutes, or until the bread is crisp and the cheese melts.

PER SERVING: Calories: 501; Total Fat: 18g; Protein: 48g; Carbohydrates: 35g; Sugars: 4g; Fiber: 5g; Sodium: 964mg

CHAPTER 7

Mains

Cauliflower Tofu Fried Rice

30 MINUTES, DAIRY-FREE, GLUTEN-FREE, ONE-POT, VEGETARIAN

SERVES 4 / PREP TIME: 10 MINUTES / COOK TIME: 15 MINUTES

If you order a side of fried rice at a restaurant, you'll set yourself back at least 500 calories, 70-plus grams of carbohydrates, and 15-plus grams of fat. This version gives you a bigger portion for only a fraction of the calories.

1 tablespoon sesame oil

8 cups riced cauliflower

12 ounces extra-firm tofu, drained and cubed

2 tablespoons tamari

¼ cup rice wine vinegar

1 bunch scallions, green and white parts, chopped

1 cup shelled edamame

1 cup frozen peas and carrots, thawed

4 large eggs, scrambled

1 tablespoon sesame seeds

Freshly ground black pepper

1. In a large skillet over medium heat, heat the sesame oil. Add the cauliflower and tofu and sauté for 5 minutes.

2. Stir in the tamari, vinegar, scallions, edamame, peas and carrots, eggs, and sesame seeds. Season with pepper. Sauté for 3 minutes.

3. Reduce the heat to the lowest setting and cook for 3 to 5 minutes until the eggs are cooked through and vegetables are soft and heated.

INGREDIENT TIPS: You can buy cauliflower already in rice form (fresh or frozen), or you can make your own. Cut one cauliflower head into florets, add them to a food processor or blender, and pulse until you achieve a rice-like texture.

If gluten sensitivity is a problem, always check the packaging to ensure ingredients were processed in a completely gluten-free facility.

SUBSTITUTION TIP: If you don't have tamari, use soy sauce instead, but remember it contains gluten. To make this dish vegan, omit the eggs.

PER SERVING: Calories: 310; Total Fat: 15g; Protein: 25g; Carbohydrates: 23g; Sugars: 9g; Fiber: 9g; Sodium: 576mg

Tuscan Pesto and White Bean Pasta

30 MINUTES, GLUTEN-FREE, VEGETARIAN

SERVES 4 / PREP TIME: 10 MINUTES / COOK TIME: 10 MINUTES

Chickpea pasta is a great alternative to regular pasta. Not only is it gluten free, but it's also higher in fiber and protein than wheat pasta. You can find it at most grocery stores. This recipe packs even more fiber thanks to the cannellini beans.

8 ounces dried chickpea pasta

1 tablespoon olive oil

3 garlic cloves, minced

1½ cups cherry tomatoes, halved

½ cup Avocado Basil Pesto (page 134)

Salt

Freshly ground black pepper

2 cups fresh baby spinach

2 cups canned cannellini beans, drained and rinsed

3 ounces Parmesan cheese, grated

1. Fill a large pot with water and bring it to a boil. Add the pasta and cook according to the package directions. Drain the pasta in a colander.

2. Meanwhile, in a large skillet over medium-low heat, heat the olive oil. Add the garlic and sauté for 1 to 2 minutes, or until it softens.

3. Add the tomatoes and pesto and season with salt and pepper. Sauté for 3 to 5 minutes until the tomatoes begin to burst.

4. Add the spinach and cook for 2 to 3 minutes, stirring until it begins to wilt.

5. Add the beans to the skillet. Cook for 3 to 5 minutes, stirring, until they are heated. The tomatoes will create a thick sauce in the skillet.

6. Add the pasta to the skillet and toss until everything is well combined. Top with the Parmesan.

INGREDIENT TIPS: If you can't find chickpea pasta, substitute black bean pasta, whole-wheat pasta, spaghetti squash, or zucchini noodles.

If gluten sensitivity is a problem, always check the packaging to ensure ingredients were processed in a completely gluten-free facility.

SERVING TIP: This pasta dish can be served hot or cold, as a meal or snack. This pasta will keep, refrigerated in an airtight container, for up to 2 days.

PER SERVING: Calories: 550; Total Fat: 20g; Protein: 24g; Carbohydrates: 75g; Sugars: 2g; Fiber: 13g; Sodium: 382mg

Slow Cooker Lentil Chili

DAIRY-FREE, GLUTEN-FREE, ONE-POT, VEGAN

SERVES 4 / PREP TIME: 10 MINUTES / COOK TIME: 6 HOURS

If you don't have a slow cooker, make this on the stovetop. Instead of adding the kidney beans at the end, add them with the rest of the ingredients and cook on low heat for 45 minutes.

⅔ cup dried lentils, rinsed

1 yellow onion, diced

1 red bell pepper, chopped

1 carrot, peeled and chopped

2 garlic cloves, minced

1½ teaspoons chili powder

¾ teaspoon ground cumin

¾ teaspoon smoked paprika

3 cups canned diced tomatoes, with their juices

1½ cups vegetable broth

Salt

Freshly ground black pepper

1½ cups canned red kidney beans, drained and rinsed

1. In a slow cooker, combine the lentils, onion, bell pepper, carrot, garlic, chili powder, cumin, paprika, tomatoes with their juices, and vegetable broth. Season with salt and pepper and stir well to combine.

2. Replace the lid and cook on low heat for 6 hours.

3. Add the kidney beans and stir to combine. Cook until heated through, then serve.

INGREDIENT TIP: If gluten sensitivity is a problem, always check the packaging to ensure ingredients were processed in a completely gluten-free facility.

SERVING TIP: Serve with avocado or chopped fresh cilantro. If you like a spicier chili, add chopped jalapeño pepper.

STORAGE TIP: Refrigerate leftovers in an airtight container for up to 5 days, or freeze for up to 6 months.

PER SERVING: Calories: 261; Total Fat: 3g; Protein: 20g; Carbohydrates: 41g; Sugars: 9g; Fiber: 16g; Sodium: 843mg

Salmon with Spinach and White Bean Orzo

30 MINUTES, DAIRY-FREE, GLUTEN-FREE, PESCATARIAN

SERVES 4 / PREP TIME: 10 MINUTES / COOK TIME: 20 MINUTES

Don't shy away from frozen salmon. Believe it or not, the "fresh" salmon in the grocery store's seafood counter was likely frozen and then thawed. The sooner your salmon is frozen after being caught, the fresher it will be when it gets to you. Most frozen salmon is flash frozen on the boat as soon as it's caught. This recipe takes basic salmon up a notch with fresh vegetables and high-fiber beans.

8 ounces dried orzo pasta

4 (4-ounce) salmon fillets

½ teaspoon salt, divided

¼ teaspoon freshly ground black pepper, divided

1 tablespoon olive oil

½ teaspoon red pepper flakes

3 garlic cloves, minced

5 ounces fresh baby spinach

1 cup cherry tomatoes, halved

1 cup canned cannellini beans, drained and rinsed

1 lemon, cut into wedges

1. Cook the orzo according to the package directions. Drain, rinse, and set aside.

2. Sprinkle the salmon with ¼ teaspoon of salt and ⅛ teaspoon of pepper.

3. In a large skillet over medium-high heat, heat the olive oil. Add the salmon to the skillet and cook for 3 minutes per side, or until cooked through. Remove the fish from the skillet and set aside.

4. Return the skillet to the heat and add the red pepper flakes and garlic. Sauté for 30 seconds. Add the spinach and sauté for 2 to 3 minutes until it wilts. Stir in the tomatoes, beans, and the remaining ¼ teaspoon of salt and ⅛ teaspoon of pepper. Cook for 1 minute more. Remove the skillet from the heat.

5. Add the orzo and toss to coat. Divide the orzo mixture among 4 plates and top each with salmon. Serve with lemon wedges for squeezing.

CONTINUED

INGREDIENT TIP: If gluten sensitivity is a problem, always check the packaging to ensure ingredients were processed in a completely gluten-free facility.

SUBSTITUTION TIP: Any other fish or shellfish, such as tilapia or shrimp, will substitute nicely for the salmon in this recipe.

PER SERVING: Calories: 540; Total Fat: 23g; Protein: 32g; Carbohydrates: 54g; Sugars: 5g; Fiber: 6g; Sodium: 382mg

Seared Sesame Ahi Tuna with Cabbage Slaw

DAIRY-FREE, GLUTEN-FREE, PESCATARIAN

SERVES 4 / PREP TIME: 10 MINUTES, PLUS 1 HOUR TO MARINATE THE TUNA AND MAKE THE DRESSING / COOK TIME: 5 MINUTES

This is the perfect dish to serve when entertaining. It looks super impressive but couldn't be easier to make.

FOR THE TUNA

2 tablespoons tamari

2 tablespoons freshly squeezed lime juice

1 tablespoon sesame oil

1 pound ahi tuna

⅓ cup sesame seeds, black or white

8 scallions, green and white parts, chopped

FOR THE CABBAGE SLAW

1½ tablespoons tamari

2 tablespoons rice vinegar

2 tablespoons sesame oil

¾ teaspoon grated peeled fresh ginger

1 tablespoon honey

1 garlic clove, minced

1 tablespoon sesame seeds, black or white

3 cups thinly sliced purple cabbage

2 carrots, peeled and shredded

2 scallions, green and white parts, chopped

TO MAKE THE TUNA

1. In a shallow bowl, whisk together the tamari, lime juice, and sesame oil. Add the tuna and turn to coat well. Cover the bowl and refrigerate to marinate for 1 hour.

2. Place the sesame seeds in a shallow bowl. Remove the tuna from the marinade and gently shake off any excess liquid. Discard any leftover marinade. Coat the tuna in the sesame seeds.

3. Heat a large nonstick skillet over medium-high heat. When the pan is hot, sear the tuna for 2 to 3 minutes, flipping it halfway through the cooking time. Sear it longer if you prefer it well done.

4. Thinly slice the tuna and garnish with the scallions.

TO MAKE THE CABBAGE SLAW

1. In an airtight container, combine the tamari, vinegar, sesame oil, ginger, honey, garlic, and sesame seeds. Cover the container and shake to combine. Refrigerate the dressing for at least 1 hour before making the slaw.

CONTINUED

2. In a large bowl, combine the cabbage, carrots, and scallions. Top with the dressing. Toss well to combine. Serve with the tuna.

INGREDIENT TIP: If gluten sensitivity is a problem, always check the packaging to ensure ingredients were processed in a completely gluten-free facility.

STORAGE TIP: The slaw can be kept, refrigerated in an airtight container, for up to 4 days.

SUBSTITUTION TIP: If you don't have tamari, use soy sauce instead, but remember it contains gluten.

PER SERVING: Calories: 347; Total Fat: 19g; Protein: 30g; Carbohydrates: 18g; Sugars: 9g; Fiber: 6g; Sodium: 1,896mg

Greek Spaghetti Squash with Shrimp

GLUTEN-FREE, PESCATARIAN

SERVES 3 / PREP TIME: 10 MINUTES / COOK TIME: 35 MINUTES

Spaghetti squash is a popular lower-carbohydrate and gluten-free pasta alternative. One cup of spaghetti squash contains only 40 calories and 10 grams of carbohydrate versus an equivalent serving of regular pasta that contains 200 calories and 40 grams of carbohydrate—that's a big savings!

Nonstick cooking spray

1 spaghetti squash, halved lengthwise, seeds and pulp removed

2 tablespoons olive oil, divided

1 yellow onion, chopped

1 garlic clove, minced

1½ cups diced tomatoes

1 pound peeled and deveined shrimp

Salt

Freshly ground black pepper

¾ cup crumbled feta cheese

¼ cup sliced black olives

1. Preheat the oven to 350° F. Lightly coat a baking sheet with cooking spray.

2. Place the spaghetti squash halves, cut-side down, on the prepared baking sheet. Bake for 30 minutes, or until a knife can be inserted into the squash with only a little resistance. Remove the squash from the oven and let cool.

3. While the spaghetti squash bakes, in a skillet over medium heat, heat 1 tablespoon of olive oil. Add the onion and cook for about 5 minutes until tender.

4. Add the garlic and cook for 2 to 3 minutes until fragrant. Stir in the tomatoes and cook for about 3 minutes until they are warmed.

5. Season the shrimp with salt and pepper.

6. In a separate skillet over medium-high heat, heat the remaining 1 tablespoon of olive oil. Add the shrimp and cook for 2 to 3 minutes until they are opaque and cooked through. Remove the shrimp from the pan and set aside.

CONTINUED

7. Once the squash has cooled, use a spoon to scoop the pulp into a medium bowl. Add the tomato mixture, feta, and olives. Toss to combine.

8. Top with the shrimp and serve warm.

INGREDIENT TIP: If gluten sensitivity is a problem, always check the packaging to ensure ingredients were processed in a completely gluten-free facility.

SUBSTITUTION TIP: Use any lean protein in place of shrimp, such as scallops or cubed chicken breast.

PER SERVING: Calories: 370; Total Fat: 20g; Protein: 32g; Carbohydrates: 21g; Sugars: 6g; Fiber: 2g; Sodium: 765mg

Asian Chicken Lettuce Wraps

30 MINUTES, DAIRY-FREE, ONE-POT

SERVES 4 / PREP TIME: 10 MINUTES / COOK TIME: 20 MINUTES

These wraps are a fun appetizer, or a great meal paired with rice. If you don't like romaine lettuce, use Bibb lettuce or cabbage leaves instead.

1 head romaine lettuce, leaves separated

1 teaspoon sesame oil

1 shallot, chopped

1 zucchini, diced

1 carrot, peeled and diced

8 scallions, green and white parts, chopped

1 pound extra-lean ground chicken

2 tablespoons low-sodium soy sauce

2 tablespoons hoisin sauce

1 tablespoon sweet chili sauce

1 tablespoon plum sauce, for serving (optional)

1. Trim each lettuce leaf to form a cup and place them in the refrigerator to chill.

2. In a large nonstick skillet over medium heat, heat the sesame oil.

3. Add the shallot, zucchini, carrot, and scallions and cook for 5 to 7 minutes until the vegetables begin to brown.

4. Add the chicken and use a wooden spoon to break up it into smaller pieces as it cooks.

5. Stir in the soy sauce, hoisin sauce, and chili sauce, mixing thoroughly. Cook the chicken for 8 to 10 minutes until it is no longer pink.

6. Serve the chicken and vegetables in the lettuce cups with plum sauce (if using).

SUBSTITUTION TIP: Use any lean protein in place of chicken.

PER SERVING: Calories: 212; Total Fat: 12g; Protein: 24g; Carbohydrates: 14g; Sugars: 7g; Fiber: 3g; Sodium: 575mg

White Chicken Chili

DAIRY-FREE, GLUTEN-FREE

SERVES 4 / PREP TIME: 10 MINUTES / COOK TIME: 45 MINUTES

This hearty chicken chili will warm you up on a cold night. Spice it up a bit with your favorite hot sauce before serving.

---

1 tablespoon olive oil, divided

1 pound boneless, skinless chicken breast, cubed

Salt

Freshly ground black pepper

2 onions, diced

2 garlic cloves, minced

2 teaspoons ground cumin

1 teaspoon ground coriander

1 (4-ounce) can diced green chiles, undrained

1 cup water

2 cups canned white beans, drained and rinsed

2 cups chicken broth

½ cup chopped fresh cilantro

1. In a large nonstick skillet over medium-high heat, heat 1½ teaspoons of olive oil. Season the chicken with salt and pepper and add it to the skillet. Cook for 10 to 12 minutes, stirring frequently, or until browned. Set aside.

2. In another large skillet over medium-high heat, heat the remaining 1½ teaspoons of olive oil. Add the onions and sauté for 5 to 7 minutes until tender, stirring frequently.

3. Add the garlic and sauté for 2 minutes more, stirring frequently. Stir in the cumin and coriander and sauté for 1 minute.

4. Stir in the green chiles and their liquid, reduce the heat to low, and cook for 10 minutes. Add the cooked chicken, water, beans, and broth and bring the mixture to a boil.

5. Cover the skillet and reduce the heat to medium-low. Simmer for 15 minutes. Taste and adjust the seasoning, as needed. Serve garnished with the cilantro.

INGREDIENT TIP: If gluten sensitivity is a problem, always check the packaging to ensure ingredients were processed in a completely gluten-free facility.

STORAGE TIP: Refrigerate in an airtight container for up to 3 days, or freeze for up to 3 months.

PER SERVING: Calories: 334; Total Fat: 7g; Protein: 27g; Carbohydrates: 32g; Sugars: 4g; Fiber: 11g; Sodium: 613mg

Chicken Quinoa Enchilada Bake

GLUTEN-FREE

SERVES 4 / PREP TIME: 20 MINUTES / COOK TIME: 30 MINUTES

This recipe blends delicious Southwestern flavors. You can make this dish vegetarian by swapping beans for the chicken breast.

1 pound boneless, skinless chicken breast

1 tablespoon olive oil

1 yellow onion, diced

2 garlic cloves, minced

1 teaspoon ground cumin

1 teaspoon chili powder

1 cup red enchilada sauce, divided

1 cup corn kernels

2 cups cooked quinoa

1½ cups shredded reduced-fat Cheddar cheese

¼ cup diced tomatoes, for garnish (optional)

¼ cup chopped fresh cilantro, for garnish (optional)

1. Preheat the oven to 350° F.

2. Place the chicken breasts into a saucepan and add enough water to cover them. Place the pan over high heat and bring the water to a boil. Reduce the heat to low and simmer for 10 to 12 minutes until the chicken is cooked through. Transfer the chicken to a bowl to cool. Using 2 forks, shred the cooled chicken and set aside.

3. In a large skillet over medium heat, heat the olive oil. Add the onion and garlic and sauté for about 6 minutes until tender. Stir in the cumin and chili powder. Transfer the mixture to an oven-safe casserole dish.

4. In the casserole dish, combine the chicken, corn, and all but 1 tablespoon of the enchilada sauce.

5. Stir in the quinoa and top with the Cheddar cheese.

6. Bake for 10 to 15 minutes until the cheese begins to melt.

7. Remove from the oven and drizzle with the reserved 1 tablespoon of enchilada sauce. Garnish with tomato and cilantro (if using).

INGREDIENT TIPS: Any kind of corn will work in this recipe: canned, frozen, or fresh, cut from the cob.

If gluten sensitivity is a problem, always check the packaging to ensure ingredients were processed in a completely gluten-free facility.

PER SERVING: Calories: 547; Total Fat: 23g; Protein: 45g; Carbohydrates: 42g; Sugars: 3g; Fiber: 5g; Sodium: 650mg

Chicken Shawarma Bowls

DAIRY-FREE, GLUTEN-FREE

SERVES 4 / PREP TIME: 10 MINUTES, PLUS 1 HOUR TO MARINATE / COOK TIME: 10 MINUTES

Shawarma is a Middle Eastern meat dish that is prepared on large spits. As the spits rotate, the meat slowly falls off as it cooks, yielding a very tender texture. You may not have a spit at home, but this is the next best thing.

---

1 pound boneless, skinless chicken thighs

2 teaspoons ground cumin

½ teaspoon ground turmeric

½ teaspoon salt

¼ teaspoon freshly ground black pepper

1 tablespoon olive oil

¼ cup tahini

Juice of ½ lemon

2 cups cooked quinoa

1 cup chopped cherry tomatoes

1 cucumber, chopped

¼ cup chopped fresh parsley, for garnish (optional)

1. In a plastic storage bag, combine the chicken, cumin, turmeric, salt, pepper, and olive oil. Seal the bag and massage to coat the chicken in the spices. Refrigerate to marinate for at least 1 hour.

2. In a small bowl, whisk together the tahini and lemon juice.

3. Place a large skillet over medium heat. Place the chicken in the skillet and cook for 10 to 12 minutes, or until it is cooked through, turning occasionally. Remove the chicken and cut it into strips.

4. Evenly divide the quinoa, tomatoes, and cucumber among 4 bowls and top with the chicken. Drizzle the tahini dressing over the chicken and sprinkle with parsley (if using).

INGREDIENT TIP: If gluten sensitivity is a problem, always check the packaging to ensure ingredients were processed in a completely gluten-free facility.

PREPARATION TIPS: Add minced garlic to the tahini dressing for more flavor. Since tahini tends to thicken as it sits, add water as needed to thin.

The chicken should marinate for at least 1 hour, but the longer the better. Prep it the night before you plan to make this recipe and refrigerate overnight for maximum flavor.

PER SERVING: Calories: 433; Total Fat: 19g; Protein: 32g; Carbohydrates: 36g; Sugars: 3g; Fiber: 6g; Sodium: 416mg

Stuffed Peppers with Turkey and Brown Rice

GLUTEN-FREE

SERVES 4 / PREP TIME: 10 MINUTES / COOK TIME: 30 MINUTES

Stuffed peppers are the perfect all-in-one meal. You have lean protein, vegetables, savory tomato sauce, and cheese. If you prefer a crisper pepper, skip the boiling.

4 bell peppers, any color, tops, ribs, and seeds removed

Nonstick cooking spray

1 pound extra-lean ground turkey

Salt

Freshly ground black pepper

1½ cups shredded part-skim mozzarella cheese, divided

1 cup Simple Pomodoro Sauce (page 138)

2 cups cooked brown rice

1. Preheat the oven to 350° F.

2. Fill a large pot with enough water to cover the peppers. Place it over high heat and bring the water to a boil. Add the peppers. Cook for 3 minutes and drain. Set the peppers aside in an oven-safe casserole dish.

3. Place a large skillet over medium heat and spray it with cooking spray.

4. Add the ground turkey and cook, using a wooden spoon to break it up into smaller pieces, for 8 to 10 minutes until no longer pink. Season with salt and pepper. Remove the skillet from the heat and transfer the turkey to a large bowl.

5. Add ½ cup of mozzarella, the Pomodoro sauce, and brown rice. Stir to combine. Divide the filling among the 4 peppers. Cover the peppers with aluminum foil and bake for 8 minutes. Remove the foil and bake for 15 minutes more, until the peppers are tender.

6. Sprinkle the top of each pepper with ¼ cup of mozzarella. Bake for 2 to 3 minutes more, or until the cheese melts.

INGREDIENT TIP: If gluten sensitivity is a problem, always check the packaging to ensure ingredients were processed in a completely gluten-free facility.

SUBSTITUTION TIP: Use cooked cauliflower rice, quinoa, or white rice instead of brown rice.

PER SERVING: Calories: 455; Total Fat: 18g; Protein: 40g; Carbohydrates: 38g; Sugars: 13g; Fiber: 6g; Sodium: 423mg

Maple Dijon Sheet Pan Pork Chops

DAIRY-FREE, GLUTEN-FREE

SERVES 4 / PREP TIME: 10 MINUTES / COOK TIME: 25 MINUTES

Center-cut pork loin chops are very lean. Use a meat thermometer to ensure the pork is cooked through. Pork should have an internal temperature of 145°F and should not show any pink when cut into.

---

1 pound Brussels sprouts, trimmed and halved

1¼ pounds sweet potatoes, cut into ½-inch cubes

1 shallot, chopped

8 fresh thyme sprigs

1 tablespoon olive oil

Salt

Freshly ground black pepper

¼ cup pure maple syrup

2 tablespoons Dijon mustard

2 garlic cloves, minced

4 (4-ounce) boneless center-cut pork loin chops

1. Preheat the oven to 400°F.

2. In a large bowl, toss together the Brussels sprouts, sweet potatoes, shallot, thyme, and olive oil and season with salt and pepper. Place the vegetables on a baking sheet in a single layer.

3. In a small bowl, stir together the maple syrup, mustard, and garlic. Brush the mixture onto both sides of the pork chops and reserve any remaining sauce. Nestle the pork chops among the vegetables and sprinkle with salt and pepper.

4. Bake for 10 minutes. Brush both sides of the pork chops with the remaining sauce and return the pan to the oven to cook for 10 to 15 minutes more until the meat is cooked through and has reached an internal temperature of 145° F. Serve hot.

INGREDIENT TIP: If gluten sensitivity is a problem, always check the packaging to ensure ingredients were processed in a completely gluten-free facility.

SUBSTITUTION TIP: If you do not have maple syrup, use honey instead.

PER SERVING: Calories: 350; Total Fat: 8g; Protein: 32g; Carbohydrates: 40g; Sugars: 9g; Fiber: 9g; Sodium: 289mg

Beef Barley Soup

DAIRY-FREE, ONE-POT

SERVES 4 / PREP TIME: 15 MINUTES / COOK TIME: 1 HOUR, 45 MINUTES

This soup is a complete meal in one bowl. With lean protein, veggies, and high-fiber grains, you get everything you need in one delicious dish.

1 teaspoon olive oil

1 pound boneless beef chuck, cubed

1 cup chopped carrots

½ cup chopped yellow onion

½ cup chopped celery

1 teaspoon kosher salt

Freshly ground black pepper

2 garlic cloves, chopped

6 cups beef broth

1½ teaspoons Worcestershire sauce

2 bay leaves

¾ cup uncooked barley

½ cup peas

1. In a large pot or Dutch oven over medium heat, heat the olive oil. Add the beef and cook for about 10 minutes, stirring occasionally, until seared on all sides. Transfer the beef to a plate.

2. In the same pot, combine the carrots, onion, celery, and salt and cook for 5 minutes, or until soft. Season with pepper. Add the garlic and cook for 2 minutes more.

3. Return the beef to the pot and add the broth, Worcestershire sauce, and bay leaves.

4. Bring the soup to a boil, then reduce the heat to a simmer. Cover the pot and simmer for 45 to 60 minutes until the beef is tender.

5. Add the barley and simmer for 30 minutes more, until softened.

6. Remove and discard the bay leaves. Stir in the peas. Cook for 3 minutes to warm the peas. Serve hot.

INGREDIENT TIP: Any kind of peas will work in this recipe: canned, frozen, or fresh from the pods.

SUBSTITUTION TIP: To make this gluten free, omit the Worcestershire sauce.

PER SERVING: Calories: 368; Total Fat: 9g; Protein: 37g; Carbohydrates: 35g; Sugars: 5g; Fiber: 8g; Sodium: 725mg

Simple Shepherd's Pie

GLUTEN-FREE

SERVES 4 / PREP TIME: 15 MINUTES / COOK TIME: 1 HOUR

Traditional shepherd's pie is made with ground beef or lamb, mixed with a heavy gravy, and topped with mashed potatoes. This healthier twist uses cauliflower mixed with the potato to add volume without sacrificing flavor or texture.

12 ounces russet potatoes, peeled and cubed

3 cups cauliflower florets

4 cups frozen mixed vegetables (peas, corn, green beans, and carrots), thawed

1 cup beef gravy

Nonstick cooking spray

1 pound extra-lean ground beef

1 tablespoon dried minced onion

Salt

Freshly ground black pepper

¼ cup reduced-fat cream cheese

1 teaspoon garlic powder

1. Preheat the oven to 375° F.

2. Bring a medium pot of water to a boil over high heat. Add the potatoes and cauliflower and return the water to a boil. Reduce the heat to medium and cook for 15 to 20 minutes, or until the vegetables are very tender.

3. Meanwhile, in a large bowl, stir together the mixed vegetables and gravy until fully coated.

4. Spray a large oven-safe skillet with cooking spray and place it over medium-high heat. Add the ground beef and minced onion and season with salt and pepper. Cook, using a wooden spoon to break up the ground beef into smaller pieces, for about 5 minutes, or until fully cooked.

5. Evenly top the beef with the gravy-coated vegetables and remove the skillet from the heat.

6. Drain the potatoes and cauliflower and transfer to a large bowl. Add the cream cheese and garlic powder and thoroughly mash and mix. Spoon the mixture onto the beef and vegetables and smooth out the top.

7. Transfer the skillet to the oven and bake for about 35 minutes until the filling begins to bubble and the top has slightly browned.

INGREDIENT TIP: If gluten sensitivity is a problem, always check the packaging to ensure ingredients were processed in a completely gluten-free facility.

SUBSTITUTION TIP: Use any lean protein in place of beef, such as ground turkey or chicken.

PER SERVING: Calories: 381; Total Fat: 8g; Protein: 31g; Carbohydrates: 45g; Sugars: 9g; Fiber: 11g; Sodium: 344mg

Sheet Pan Steak Fajitas

30 MINUTES, DAIRY-FREE, GLUTEN-FREE

SERVES 4 / PREP TIME: 10 MINUTES / COOK TIME: 20 MINUTES

This is the perfect family meal. Put out an array of fun toppings so everyone can make the meal their own!

FOR THE SEASONING

2 teaspoons chili powder

1 teaspoon ground cumin

1 teaspoon garlic powder

1 teaspoon paprika

½ teaspoon salt

¼ teaspoon freshly ground black pepper

FOR THE STEAK

8 corn tortillas

1 pound flank steak, cut into ½-inch strips

1 large sweet onion, sliced

1 red bell pepper, sliced

1 green bell pepper, sliced

1 tablespoon olive oil

Juice of 1 lime

TO MAKE THE SEASONING

In a small bowl, stir together the chili powder, cumin, garlic powder, paprika, salt, and pepper until evenly mixed. Set aside.

TO MAKE THE STEAK

1. Preheat the oven to 400°F. Line a baking sheet with aluminum foil and set aside.

2. Wrap the tortillas in foil and set aside.

3. In a large bowl, combine the steak, onion, and bell peppers. Drizzle with the olive oil and lime juice. Mix until well coated. Sprinkle the seasoning over the steak and vegetables and stir again until evenly coated. Transfer the meat and vegetables to the prepared baking sheet and spread in a single layer.

4. Bake for 12 to 20 minutes, or until the steak reaches your desired doneness. Place the tortillas in the oven to warm at the same time. Remove tortillas after about 5 minutes.

5. Fill each warm tortilla with even portions of the steak, vegetable filling, and any desired toppings.

INGREDIENT TIP: If gluten sensitivity is a problem, always check the packaging to ensure ingredients were processed in a completely gluten-free facility.

SERVING TIP: Serve with lime wedges for squeezing, fresh cilantro for garnishing, and your favorite toppings, such as salsa or sour cream.

SUBSTITUTION TIP: Use any lean protein in place of the steak, such as chicken strips or salmon.

PER SERVING: Calories: 380; Total Fat: 16g; Protein: 29g; Carbohydrates: 33g; Sugars: 6g; Fiber: 6g; Sodium: 330mg

Desserts

Baked Cinnamon Apples

DAIRY-FREE, GLUTEN-FREE, VEGAN

SERVES 4 / PREP TIME: 5 MINUTES / COOK TIME: 30 MINUTES

Top these warm apples with something creamy (see serving tip) and you have a decadent but healthy dessert. Any sweet apple, such as Fuji, Honeycrisp, Pink Lady, or Gala, will work.

4 apples

1 tablespoon coconut oil, at room temperature

1 tablespoon light brown sugar

½ teaspoon ground cinnamon

½ cup old-fashioned rolled oats

1. Preheat the oven to 350°F.

2. Cut a slice from the stem end of the apple. Using an apple corer or a melon baller, remove the core, but leave the base intact so it can hold the filling. Place the cored apples into a baking dish. (If the apples do not sit flat, remove a thin slice from the bottom of each.)

3. In a small bowl, stir together the coconut oil, brown sugar, cinnamon, and oats. Sprinkle the mixture into the center of the apples. Fill the baking dish ½ inch of water. Gently cover the apples with aluminum foil.

4. Bake for 30 minutes, or until the apples are tender.

INGREDIENT TIP: If gluten sensitivity is a problem, always check the packaging to ensure ingredients were processed in a completely gluten-free facility.

SERVING TIP: Serve the apples warm with a scoop of vanilla Greek yogurt, dairy-free whipped topping, or a light vanilla ice cream.

PER SERVING: Calories: 192; Total Fat: 5g; Protein: 2g; Carbohydrates: 40g; Sugars: 26g; Fiber: 7g; Sodium: 3mg

Apple Nachos

30 MINUTES, DAIRY-FREE, GLUTEN-FREE, ONE-POT, VEGETARIAN

SERVES 4 / PREP TIME: 10 MINUTES

There are endless varieties of apple nachos you can make with this simple recipe. Experiment with your favorite toppings, like any nut butter, a sprinkle or two of cinnamon or nutmeg, or even melted cheese, to make this dish your own. Any sweet apple, such as Fuji, Honeycrisp, Pink Lady, or Gala, will work well as "nachos."

2 apples, cored and cut into ¼-inch slices

2 tablespoons honey

¼ cup dark chocolate chips

2 tablespoons chopped peanuts

1. Arrange the apple slices on a serving plate.

2. Drizzle the honey over the apple slices.

3. Top with chocolate chips and peanuts.

INGREDIENT TIP: If gluten sensitivity is a problem, always check the packaging to ensure ingredients were processed in a completely gluten-free facility.

PER SERVING: Calories: 151; Total Fat: 5g; Protein: 2g; Carbohydrates: 30g; Sugars: 24g; Fiber: 3g; Sodium: 2mg

Banana Raspberry Nice Cream

30 MINUTES, DAIRY-FREE, GLUTEN-FREE, ONE-POT, VEGAN

SERVES 4 / PREP TIME: 5 MINUTES

It doesn't get any easier than this four-ingredient recipe. Play around with the flavors; just make sure you don't omit the bananas, as they hold the recipe together.

4 bananas, frozen

½ cup unsweetened vanilla almond milk, divided

1 cup frozen raspberries

2 tablespoons dark chocolate chips

1. In a high-speed blender or food processor, combine the bananas and ¼ cup of almond milk. Blend on high speed for 1 to 2 minutes, stopping to scrape down the sides, as needed.

2. Add the raspberries and chocolate chips and blend for 1 to 2 minutes.

3. Add the remaining ¼ cup of almond milk, as needed, to thin the mixture. Once the ingredients are puréed, they should resemble a very thick smoothie. Eat immediately or freeze for 1 to 2 hours so the mixture hardens.

INGREDIENT TIP: If gluten sensitivity is a problem, always check the packaging to ensure ingredients were processed in a completely gluten-free facility.

STORAGE TIP: Freeze in an airtight glass container. Thaw in the refrigerator for 30 minutes before serving.

SUBSTITUTION TIP: Substitute any frozen fruit in place of the raspberries.

PER SERVING: Calories: 144; Total Fat: 2g; Protein: 2g; Carbohydrates: 33g; Sugars: 18g; Fiber: 5g; Sodium: 24mg

Avocado Chocolate Mousse

30 MINUTES, DAIRY-FREE, GLUTEN-FREE, ONE-POT, VEGAN

SERVES 4 / PREP TIME: 10 MINUTES

Adding avocado to chocolate mousse adds creaminess without the calories. You won't even notice the subtle taste of the avocado (you will, however, notice the insanely creamy texture!). Use very ripe avocados for this recipe.

2 avocados, halved and pitted

4 ounces dark baking chocolate, melted

3 tablespoons unsweetened cocoa powder

⅓ cup unsweetened vanilla almond milk

2 tablespoons maple syrup

½ teaspoon vanilla extract

¼ teaspoon ground cinnamon

⅛ teaspoon salt

1. Scoop the avocado flesh into a food processor or a high-speed blender.

2. Add the baking chocolate, cocoa powder, almond milk, maple syrup, vanilla, cinnamon, and salt. Purée until smooth.

3. Spoon the chocolate mousse into four ramekins and chill for at least 1 hour before serving.

INGREDIENT TIP: If gluten sensitivity is a problem, always check the packaging to ensure ingredients were processed in a completely gluten-free facility.

SERVING TIP: Top with cacao nibs for a nice crunch.

STORAGE TIP: The mousse will keep, refrigerated in an airtight container, for up to 4 days.

PER SERVING: Calories: 325; Total Fat: 23g; Protein: 3g; Carbohydrates: 35g; Sugars: 20g; Fiber: 8g; Sodium: 107mg

Black Bean Brownies

DAIRY-FREE, GLUTEN-FREE, VEGETARIAN

SERVES 9 / PREP TIME: 10 MINUTES / COOK TIME: 35 MINUTES, PLUS 4 HOURS TO CHILL

Adding black beans to these brownies creates a smooth and creamy texture. No one will ever know these gooey brownies were made with a high-fiber secret ingredient.

1 (15-ounce) can black beans, drained and rinsed

3 large eggs

¼ cup coconut oil, melted

¾ cup cocoa powder

¼ cup sugar

¼ cup honey

½ teaspoon baking powder

¼ teaspoon salt

1 teaspoon vanilla extract

½ cup dark chocolate chips, divided

1. Preheat the oven to 350° F. Line an 8-by-8-inch baking dish with parchment paper and set aside.

2. In a food processor, combine the black beans and eggs. Pulse to combine. With the processor running, stream in the coconut oil. Blend for 1 minute, or until smooth.

3. Add the cocoa powder, sugar, honey, salt, baking powder, and vanilla. Blend until the ingredients are incorporated, scraping down the sides of the processor, as needed.

4. Add ¼ cup of chocolate chips and pulse 5 or 6 times until the chocolate is mixed in. Pour the batter into the prepared baking dish and smooth the top. Sprinkle the remaining ¼ cup of chocolate chips over the top of the brownies.

5. Bake for 30 to 35 minutes, or until a toothpick inserted into the center comes out clean.

6. Let the brownies cool completely before transferring them to the refrigerator. Chill for at least 4 hours before cutting into squares.

INGREDIENT TIP: If gluten sensitivity is a problem, always check the packaging to ensure ingredients were processed in a completely gluten-free facility.

STORAGE TIP: These brownies keep well, refrigerated, for up to 4 days.

PER SERVING: Calories: 241; Total Fat: 11g; Protein: 8g; Carbohydrates: 34g; Sugars: 17g; Fiber: 7g; Sodium: 92mg

Grain-Free Chocolate Chunk Cookies

30 MINUTES, DAIRY-FREE, GLUTEN-FREE, VEGETARIAN

SERVES 12 / PREP TIME: 10 MINUTES / COOK TIME: 15 MINUTES

Cookies are typically made with all-purpose flour. In this recipe, you use almond flour and coconut flour to decrease the carbohydrate content and increase the fiber!

1 large egg, slightly beaten

¼ cup olive oil

½ cup sugar

1 teaspoon vanilla extract

1 cup almond flour

¼ cup coconut flour

½ teaspoon baking soda

3 ounces dark chocolate, chopped

¼ cup unsweetened vanilla almond milk, or less, for moisture

Coarse sea salt, for garnish

1. Preheat the oven to 350° F.

2. In a large bowl, whisk together the egg, olive oil, sugar, and vanilla.

3. Add the almond flour, coconut flour, and baking soda. Whisk well to combine until a dough forms.

4. Fold in the chocolate.

5. Stir in the almond milk, as needed, to moisten the dough. Use a spoon to drop the dough onto a baking sheet. Gently flatten each cookie with the back of the spoon.

6. Bake for 11 to 13 minutes, or until the edges of the cookies are slightly brown.

7. Sprinkle the cookies with sea salt. Let cool on the baking sheet for 10 minutes before transferring to a wire rack to cool completely.

INGREDIENT TIPS: Look for chocolate that is at least 70 percent cocoa.

If gluten sensitivity is a problem, always check the packaging to ensure ingredients were processed in a completely gluten-free facility.

SUBSTITUTION TIP: To make vegan cookies, use a flax egg: In a small bowl, stir together 1 tablespoon ground flaxseed and 3 tablespoons hot (just boiled) water. Let the mixture sit for 2 minutes before using.

PER SERVING: Calories: 162; Total Fat: 10g; Protein: 3g; Carbohydrates: 17g; Sugars: 12g; Fiber: 3g; Sodium: 63mg

Dark Chocolate Strawberry Bites

30 MINUTES, DAIRY-FREE, GLUTEN-FREE, VEGAN

SERVES 4 / PREP TIME: 5 MINUTES / COOK TIME: 10 MINUTES

This fun take on chocolate-covered strawberries is the perfect sweet treat for after dinner! They're delicious topped with crushed hazelnuts, too.

4 ounces dark chocolate

4 fresh strawberries, stemmed and sliced

2 tablespoons slivered almonds

1. Spread a large piece of wax paper on a flat surface.

2. Fill a large pot with water and place a smaller pot or heatproof bowl inside. Place the double boiler over high heat and bring the water to a boil. Reduce the heat to a simmer. Ensure that no water gets into the smaller pot.

3. Add the dark chocolate to the smaller pot and heat, stirring continuously, until the chocolate melts. Spoon the chocolate onto the wax paper into four even circles.

4. Immediately place one sliced strawberry in the center of each chocolate disk and sprinkle with the almonds.

5. Let the chocolate cool for 1 hour before peeling the coated strawberries off the wax paper.

INGREDIENT TIPS: Look for chocolate that is at least 70 percent cocoa.

If gluten sensitivity is a problem, always check the packaging to ensure ingredients were processed in a completely gluten-free facility.

PREPARATION TIP: To speed the process, heat the chocolate in a microwave-safe container for 20 seconds, then stir. If needed, microwave for 20 seconds more and stir.

STORAGE TIP: Freeze these in an airtight container. Let thaw for 10 minutes before eating them.

PER SERVING: Calories: 144; Total Fat: 10g; Protein: 2g; Carbohydrates: 19g; Sugars: 15g; Fiber: 3g; Sodium: 10mg

Grilled Peaches with Ricotta and Honey

30 MINUTES, GLUTEN-FREE, ONE-POT, VEGETARIAN

SERVES 4 / PREP TIME: 5 MINUTES / COOK TIME: 10 MINUTES

As if fresh summer peaches weren't delicious enough on their own, watch what happens when you grill them and they start to caramelize.

1 cup part-skim ricotta

½ teaspoon ground cinnamon

2 tablespoons honey

2 peaches, halved and pitted

1. In a small bowl, whisk together the ricotta, cinnamon, and honey. Cover the bowl and refrigerate.

2. Preheat a grill to medium-high heat or place a grill pan over medium-high heat. Grill the peaches, cut-side down, for 3 to 5 minutes per side until they soften and develop a char.

3. Top the peaches with the ricotta mixture and serve.

INGREDIENT TIP: If gluten sensitivity is a problem, always check the packaging to ensure ingredients were processed in a completely gluten-free facility.

PER SERVING: Calories: 148; Total Fat: 5g; Protein: 8g; Carbohydrates: 19g; Sugars: 16g; Fiber: 1g; Sodium: 78mg

Cheesecake-Stuffed Strawberries

30 MINUTES, VEGETARIAN

SERVES 4 / PREP TIME: 15 MINUTES

If you like no-bake recipes, you're going to love this sweet yet tangy dessert. Fresh figs are also a great alternative to strawberries in this recipe.

---

12 fresh strawberries

⅓ cup whipped cream cheese, at room temperature

1 tablespoon honey

½ teaspoon vanilla extract

2 tablespoons graham cracker crumbs

1. Trim the strawberries to remove the hull as well as some of the flesh to create a hollow space for the filling.

2. In a small bowl, stir together the cream cheese, honey, and vanilla until well mixed. Transfer the cream cheese mixture to a piping bag (or a plastic bag with a bottom corner snipped off). Pipe a small amount of cream cheese into each strawberry.

3. Sprinkle the tops with graham cracker crumbs.

PREPARATION TIP: If using whole graham crackers, finely crush them in a food processor or place them in a resealable bag and roll with a rolling pin.

PER SERVING: Calories: 86; Total Fat: 5g; Protein: 1g; Carbohydrates: 10g; Sugars: 7g; Fiber: 1g; Sodium: 66mg

Peanut Butter Energy Balls

DAIRY-FREE, GLUTEN-FREE, VEGETARIAN

SERVES 4 / PREP TIME: 10 MINUTES, PLUS 1½ HOURS TO CHILL

These are perfect for an after-dinner treat or afternoon snack and will satisfy your sweet tooth plus give you a little energy boost. They are so delicious you may end up nibbling on a few while making them, which is fine—as long as it's snack time.

¾ cup old-fashioned rolled oats

¼ cup creamy peanut butter

½ overripe banana, mashed

2 tablespoons honey

2 tablespoons unsweetened coconut flakes

2 tablespoons dark chocolate chips

1 tablespoon chia seeds

½ teaspoon vanilla extract

1. Line a baking sheet with parchment paper and set aside.

2. In a large bowl, stir together the oats, peanut butter, banana, honey, coconut flakes, chocolate chips, chia seeds, and vanilla until well combined. Refrigerate the mixture for 1 hour.

3. Take the dough out of the refrigerator and roll it into balls, about 1 tablespoon each. Place them on the prepared baking sheet and refrigerate for at least 30 minutes before serving.

INGREDIENT TIP: If gluten sensitivity is a problem, always check the packaging to ensure ingredients were processed in a completely gluten-free facility.

STORAGE TIP: Refrigerate in an airtight container for up to 3 days.

PER SERVING: Calories: 279; Total Fat: 15g; Protein: 8g; Carbohydrates: 31g; Sugars: 15g; Fiber: 5g; Sodium: 79mg

Sauces and Dressings

Avocado Basil Pesto

SERVES 4 / PREP TIME: 10 MINUTES

Pesto might look innocent, but traditional varieties can pack a ton of fat and calories. This lightened-up version uses less olive oil and adds avocado to keep the flavor—without the exorbitant calorie count.

½ avocado, pitted

3 cups fresh basil leaves

¼ cup grated Parmesan cheese

2 garlic cloves, peeled

Juice of ½ lemon

2 tablespoons low-sodium vegetable broth, plus more as needed

2 teaspoons olive oil

1. Scoop the avocado flesh into a high-speed blender or food processor.

2. Add the basil, Parmesan, garlic, lemon juice, broth, and olive oil. Blend or pulse until the pesto is smooth and well combined. Add more broth, if needed, to thin the pesto.

INGREDIENT TIP: If gluten sensitivity is a problem, always check the packaging to ensure ingredients were processed in a completely gluten-free facility.

PER SERVING: Calories: 124; Total Fat: 11g; Protein: 4g; Carbohydrates: 6g; Sugars: 0g; Fiber: 4g; Sodium: 82mg

Green Goddess Dressing

30 MINUTES, GLUTEN-FREE, VEGAN

SERVES 4 / PREP TIME: 10 MINUTES

Use this as a dressing for your favorite salad or as a healthy dip for crudités at your next party. It's delicious with the BLT Chopped Salad (page 82).

½ cup fresh basil leaves

⅓ cup water

¼ avocado

2 scallions, root ends trimmed

1½ tablespoons apple cider vinegar

1 tablespoon chopped yellow onion

1 tablespoon chopped fresh parsley

1 garlic clove

2 teaspoons olive oil

1 teaspoon chopped fresh chives

¼ teaspoon salt

⅛ teaspoon freshly ground black pepper

In a high-speed blender or food processor, combine the basil, water, avocado, scallions, vinegar, onion, parsley, garlic, olive oil, chives, salt, and pepper. Blend until well combined.

INGREDIENT TIP: If gluten sensitivity is a problem, always check the packaging to ensure ingredients were processed in a completely gluten-free facility.

STORAGE TIP: Refrigerate in an airtight container for up to 1 week. Shake well before using.

PER SERVING: Calories: 52; Total Fat: 5g; Protein: 1g; Carbohydrates: 2g; Sugars: 0g; Fiber: 1g; Sodium: 150mg

Light Caesar Dressing

30 MINUTES, PESCATARIAN

SERVES 4 / PREP TIME: 10 MINUTES

On its own, Caesar salad is fairly benign—but add the creamy dressing and your romaine lettuce quickly turns into a calorie bomb. This Light Caesar Dressing is still creamy, but the Greek yogurt keeps the calories and fat down.

⅓ cup grated Parmesan cheese

¼ cup plain nonfat Greek yogurt

¼ cup freshly squeezed lemon juice

1 garlic clove, minced

2 teaspoons Dijon mustard

2 anchovy fillets, mashed

1 tablespoon olive oil

1 teaspoon Worcestershire sauce

Salt

Freshly ground black pepper

In a small bowl, combine the Parmesan, yogurt, lemon juice, garlic, mustard, anchovies, olive oil, and Worcestershire sauce. Whisk until smooth. Taste and season with salt and pepper, as needed.

PREPARATION TIP: To make this in a blender, combine all the ingredients, except the salt and pepper, and pulse several times until smooth. Season as needed.

SUBSTITUTION TIP: To make this gluten free, omit the Worcestershire sauce.

PER SERVING: Calories: 92; Total Fat: 7g; Protein: 7g; Carbohydrates: 2g; Sugars: 1g; Fiber: 0g; Sodium: 617mg

Sesame Ginger Dressing

30 MINUTES, DAIRY-FREE, ONE-POT, VEGAN

SERVES 4 / PREP TIME: 10 MINUTES

Use this dressing on your favorite salad or slaw (like Seared Sesame Ahi Tuna with Cabbage Slaw on page 105 instead of the dressing in the recipe) or as a marinade for meat or tofu.

¼ cup rice wine vinegar

3 tablespoons low-sodium soy sauce

2 tablespoons sesame oil

1 tablespoon agave nectar

1 tablespoon peanut butter

1 tablespoon minced peeled fresh ginger

2 garlic cloves, minced

In a medium bowl, whisk the vinegar, soy sauce, sesame oil, agave, peanut butter, ginger, and garlic until well combined.

STORAGE TIP: Refrigerate in an airtight container for up to 7 days.

SUBSTITUTION TIP: To make this gluten free, use tamari in place of the soy sauce.

PER SERVING: Calories: 123; Total Fat: 9g; Protein: 2g; Carbohydrates: 7g; Sugars: 4g; Fiber: 1g; Sodium: 469mg

Simple Pomodoro Sauce

DAIRY-FREE, GLUTEN-FREE, ONE-POT, VEGAN

SERVES 4 / PREP TIME: 10 MINUTES / COOK TIME: 45 MINUTES

No need to turn to a jarred sauce, which can pack a ton of hidden sugar and salt—this simple tomato sauce is great to keep in the freezer for a rainy day.

---

1 tablespoon olive oil

1 yellow onion, diced

2 garlic cloves, minced

1 (32-ounce) can whole tomatoes, with their juices

8 fresh basil leaves

1 teaspoon dried oregano

¼ teaspoon red pepper flakes

Salt

Freshly ground black pepper

1. In a medium saucepan over medium heat, heat the olive oil. Add the onion and garlic and sauté for 2 to 3 minutes until the onion is translucent.

2. Add the tomatoes with their juices, using a wooden spoon to break them up as you stir.

3. Stir in the basil, oregano, and red pepper flakes and season with salt and pepper.

4. Bring the sauce to a boil. Reduce the heat to a simmer and cook for 45 minutes, stirring occasionally.

INGREDIENT TIP: If gluten sensitivity is a problem, always check the packaging to ensure ingredients were processed in a completely gluten-free facility.

STORAGE TIP: Refrigerate the sauce in an airtight container for up to 4 days, or freeze for up to 6 months.

PER SERVING: Calories: 86; Total Fat: 4g; Protein: 3g; Carbohydrates: 12g; Sugars: 7g; Fiber: 4g; Sodium: 51mg

Measurement Conversions

VOLUME EQUIVALENTS (LIQUID)

US STANDARD	US STANDARD (OUNCES)	METRIC (APPROXIMATE)
2 tablespoons	1 fl. oz.	30 mL
¼ cup	2 fl. oz.	60 mL
½ cup	4 fl. oz.	120 mL
1 cup	8 fl. oz.	240 mL
1½ cups	12 fl. oz.	355 mL
2 cups or 1 pint	16 fl. oz.	475 mL
4 cups or 1 quart	32 fl. oz.	1 L
1 gallon	128 fl. oz.	4 L

OVEN TEMPERATURES

FAHRENHEIT	CELSIUS (APPROXIMATE)
250°F	120°C
300°F	150°C
325°F	165°C
350°F	180°C
375°F	190°C
400°F	200°C
425°F	220°C
450°F	230°C

VOLUME EQUIVALENTS (DRY)

US. STANDARD	METRIC (APPROXIMATE)
⅛ teaspoon	0.5 mL
¼ teaspoon	1 mL
½ teaspoon	2 mL
¾ teaspoon	4 mL
1 teaspoon	5 mL
1 tablespoon	15 mL
¼ cup	59 mL
⅓ cup	79 mL
½ cup	118 mL
⅔ cup	156 mL
¾ cup	177 mL
1 cup	235 mL
2 cups or 1 pint	475 mL
3 cups	700 mL
4 cups or 1 quart	1 L

WEIGHT EQUIVALENTS

US STANDARD	METRIC (APPROXIMATE)
½ ounce	15 g
1 ounce	30 g
2 ounces	60 g
4 ounces	115 g
8 ounces	225 g
12 ounces	340 g
16 ounces or 1 pound	455 g

Starchy and Nonstarchy Vegetables

There are two types of vegetables: starchy and nonstarchy.

STARCHY VEGETABLES

These vegetables are great sources of vitamins, minerals, and fiber but they do contain more carbohydrates than nonstarchy veggies. Although these foods can absolutely be part of a healthy diet, you want to be more careful with portions than with nonstarchy vegetables.

- Acorn squash
- Butternut squash
- Corn
- Green peas
- Parsnips
- Plantains
- Potato
- Pumpkin

NONSTARCHY VEGETABLES

Nonstarchy vegetables also provide vitamins, minerals, and fiber but have fewer carbs.

1 cup of raw (about ½ cup cooked) nonstarchy vegetables contain about 25 calories and less than 5 grams of carbs.

- Artichoke/ Artichoke hearts
- Asparagus
- Baby corn
- Bamboo shoots
- Beans (green, wax, Italian)
- Bean sprouts
- Beets
- Broccoli
- Brussels sprouts
- Cabbage (green, red)
- Carrots
- Cauliflower

- Celery
- Coleslaw
  (no dressing)
- Cucumber
- Daikon
- Eggplant
- Greens
  (collard, kale,
  mustard, turnip)
- Hearts of palm
- Jicama
- Kohlrabi
- Leeks

- Mushrooms
- Okra
- Onions
- Pea pods
- Peppers
- Radishes
- Rutabaga
- Salad greens
  (chicory, endive,
  escarole, lettuce,
  romaine, spinach,
  arugula, radicchio,
  watercress)

- Sprouts
- Squash
  (crookneck,
  cushaw, spa-
  ghetti, summer,
  zucchini)
- Sugar snap peas
- Swiss chard
- Tomato
- Turnips
- Water chestnuts
- Yard-long beans

Resources

MyFitnessPal (www.myfitnesspal.com): Use this app to track calories and micronutrients.

Healthline (www.healthline.com): This website is devoted to science-backed, evidence-based health and nutrition information.

TDEE Calculator (https://tdeecalculator.net): Use the TDEE calculator to calculate your total daily energy expenditure. From there, you can figure out how many calories you need to eat for weight loss.

Thrive Market (www.thrivemarket.com): Visit this online market for high-quality, healthy, and sustainable products at affordable prices.

References

Aron-Wisnewsky, J., and K. Clément. "The Gut Microbiome, Diet, and Links to Cardiometabolic and Chronic Disorders." *Nature Reviews. Nephrology* 12, no. 3 (March 2016): 169–81. doi:10.1038/nrneph.2015.191.

Cappuccio, Francesco P., Frances M. Taggart, Ngianga-Bakwin Kandala, Andrew Currie, Ed Peile, Saverio Stranges, and Michelle A. Miller. "Meta-Analysis of Short Sleep Duration and Obesity in Children and Adults." *Sleep* 31, no. 5 (May 1, 2008): 619–626. doi:10.1093/sleep/31.5.619

Cummings, J. H., and G. T. Macfarlane. "Role of Intestinal Bacteria in Nutrient Metabolism." *JPEN. Journal of Parental and Enteral Nutrition* 21, no. 6 (Nov–Dec 1997): 357–65. doi:10.1177/0148607197021006357.

Després, Jean-Pierre. "Health Consequences of Visceral Obesity." *Annals of Medicine 33*, no. 8 (2001): 534–41. https://doi.org/10.3109/07853890108995963.

Distrutti, Eleonora, Lorenzo Monaldi, Patrizia Ricci, and Stefano Fiorucci. "Gut Microbiota Role in Irritable Bowel Syndrome: New Therapeutic Strategies." *World Journal of Gastroenterology* 22, no. 7 (February 21, 2016): 2219–2241. doi:10.3748/wjg.v22.i7.2219.

Fu, J., M. J. Bonder, M. C. Cenit, E. F. Tigchelaar, A. Maatman, J. A. Dekens, E. Brandsma, et al. "The Gut Microbiome Contributes to a Substantial Proportion of the Variation in Blood Lipids." *Circulation Research* 117, no. 9 (October 9, 2015): 817–24. doi:10.1161/CIRCRESAHA.115.306807.

Larsson, B., K. Svärdsudd, L. Welin, L. Wilhelmsen, P. Björntorp, and G. Tibblin. "Abdominal Adipose Tissue Distribution, Obesity, and Risk of

Cardiovascular Disease and Death: 13 Year Follow Up of Participants in the Study of Men Born in 1913." *British Medical Journal (Clinical Research Ed.)* 288, no. 6428 (1984): 1401–1404. doi:10.1136/bmj.288.6428.1401.

Ohlson, L.O., B. Larsson, K. Svärdsudd, L. Welin, H. Eriksson, L. Wilhelmsen, P. Björntorp, et al. "The Influence of Body Fat Distribution on the Incidence of Diabetes Mellitus: 13.5 Years of Follow Up of the Participants in the Study of Men Born in 1913." *Diabetes* 34, no. 10 (1985): 1055–058. doi:10.2337/diab.34.10.1055.

Smith, Steven R., Jennifer C. Lovejoy, Frank Greenway, Donna Ryan, Lilian Dejonge, Jacques De La Bretonne, Julia Volafova, et al. "Contributions of Total Body Fat, Abdominal Subcutaneous Adipose Tissue Compartments, and Visceral Adipose Tissue to the Metabolic Complications of Obesity." *Metabolism: Clinical and Experimental* 50, no. 4 (April 2001): 425–35. https://doi.org/10.1053/meta.2001.21693.

Taheri, Shahrad, Ling Lin, Diane Austin, Terry Young, and Emmanuel Mignot. "Short Sleep Duration Is Associated with Reduced Leptin, Elevated Ghrelin, and Increased Body Mass Index." *PLoS Medicine* 1, no. 3 (December 2004): e62. doi:10.1371/journal.pmed.0010062.

Zhang, Cuilin, Kathryn M. Rexrode, Rob M. van Dam, Tricia Y. Li, and Frank B. Hu. "Abdominal Obesity and the Risk of All-Cause, Cardiovascular, and Cancer Mortality." *Circulation* 117, no. 13 (2008): 1658–667. doi:10.1161/CIRCULATIONAHA.107.739714.

Zhang, Q., Y. Wu, and X. Fei. "Effect of Probiotics on Body Weight and Body-Mass Index: A Systematic Review and Meta-Analysis of Randomized, Controlled Trials." *International Journal of Food Sciences and Nutrition* 67, no. 5 (August 2015): 571–80. doi:10.108%9637486.2016.1181156.

Index

About the Author

Alix Turoff is a Registered Dietitian Nutritionist, NASM Certified Personal Trainer, and entrepreneur. She holds a bachelor's degree in Media, Culture, and Communications and Nutrition from New York University and a master's degree in Clinical Nutrition from New York University.

Alix is the founder of Alix Turoff Nutrition, where she helps clients manage their weight and heal their relationships with food through nutrition therapy. Her private practice is 100 percent virtual. She meets with clients through a HIPAA-compliant telehealth platform that allows her to see clients all over the world. She also offers courses, group programs, and in-person events.

Alix's approach to nutrition and fitness is all about finding balance. She teaches clients how to manage their weight while still enjoying a life of delicious food and drink using a "flexible dieting" approach.

To learn more, or to work with Alix, visit www.AlixTuroffNutrition.com.